Black Musicians
of America

Richard X. Donovan

National Book Company
Portland, Oregon

297059

0-89420-271-5

Table of Contents

To the Readers

No book, no matter how large or how many pages, can tell the complete story about *Black Musicians in America* — or can adequately describe the wonderful contribution they have made to American music. Although our principal objective is to pay tribute to that contribution, we also want our listing to be as complete and thorough as possible.

If you feel, in all fairness, that there are major black musicians — past or present — who should be added to this volume, please send us the name or names, along with biographical information that you feel supports their inclusion.

National Book Company
PO Box 8795
Portland OR 97207-8795

Chapter One

Origins

Chapter One

Origins

Music came first. Before humans spoke, they sang and the voice was the first musical instrument. Emotions were expressed in song before thoughts were expressed in speech. Song was both creative and an imitation of the environment. It may have been a simple cry of joy or alarm, or it may have been an effort to reproduce a birdsong or a brook, or the wind, or thunder.

But song as feeling must be understood if the pages that follow are to be understood. There is nothing so universal as music as an expression of human feeling. We must first understand it as *human*, before we can understand the many ways in which it subdivides with time and culture.

In America, a European musical culture and an African musical influence were introduced at about the same time, and both changed in the process. The evidence is very strong that the Africans who came to these shores brought their musical heritage with them.

There were several characteristics in West African music. First, it expressed a spirit that was free, and this spirit, expressed in music, has never been quenched. The other characteristic, that needed no comprehension in words, was rhythm. Even today, the African drum is a treasured possession with a heart and soul of its own. Conversations are held with drums, with a plaintive chant above it. And there is the intensity which has made Afro-American music so distinctive and appealing.

There is an Old African saying: "The spirit will not descend without a song." The saying reveals how important music was to the African soul. It also suggests that music was so powerful that it had to interact with something outside of human nature. It descended, much as the Holy Spirit of some Christian religions. The feelings generated by music were, and are, often so intense that they must be seen as coming from outside, or from above, even as something supernatural.

This feeling survives in gospel music and hymns, but in other types of music, it seems accepted that feeling comes from within, influenced by all the experience that has gone before.

Black musicians in America took the dominant musical forms and instruments and made them uniquely their own. Songs in the early slave quarters were purely African, but in time they came to be influenced by the new environment and by the natural movement away from the culture of the West African homeland.

Music was one of the few forms of expression allowed to the slaves. Even so, it was often banned, and the drum, the heartbeat of African rhythm, was particularly forbidden.

Music allowed the slaves a freedom of the spirit which survived their conditions. If it focused on sorrow, there was little cause for joy. The slave songs which arose so spontaneously from the Black soul spoke, in the beginning, of homesickness. In time, they focused on life on the plantation — on the confinement, the pain and unremitting weariness from work in the fields. Sorrow — intense sorrow — was the constant theme.

Music gave sorrow an outlet. The need and the talent gave expression to sorrow, and in time, the sorrow allowed the intrusion of moments of joy.

When all the instruments of the Black heritage were banned for so long, they tended to be lost and forgotten. With emancipation, Blacks picked up the instruments at hand, with skill and aptitude. The saxophone and other reed instruments, and horns, were most popular at first. The piano and guitar followed.

When we think of the spirit descending, it is clear that early Black musicians wanted to leave room for the descent. Almost none of them could read music, and they counted that a great blessing. The confinement of music on paper stifled their creativity and innovation, and would never have allowed the spontaneity which made their music exciting and distinctive. If the spirit descended, it could also break forth once it was within. It has been said: "Mathematical precision is not characteristic of this style; its vitality springs from the unconscious rather than the conscious mind." Perhaps we can condense this to the single word: "feeling."

West African influences have survived to this day. The work songs which preceded so many other Black musical forms, were almost purely West African in origin. The Charleston, a song and dance craze of the late 1920s and early 1930s, was a West African ancestral dance. Duke Ellington once performed a program of pure African music for a Black audience that responded with intense empathy.

The attraction of an African heritage also reveals itself in the number of Black American musicians who have visited Africa and have both listened and performed. The experience is said to be moving for both the Americans and their hosts. There is nothing more human. Americans of every origin visit their ancestral homelands, where music is often a sensitive part of the experience. If we understand music in a certain way, then all music is soul music. It requires musicians to release it in a variety of styles. Black American musicians have done this in a most natural and powerful expression.

Commentaries on Black music during the latter days of slavery are not plentiful. But there are enough to pinpoint the nature of the music which followed emancipation.

Slaves were the ancestors of the free musicians of this book. The music of slavery can still be heard as an echo of the plantation. The 19th century abolitionist, Frederick Douglass, wrote: "It is a great mistake to suppose the slaves happy because they sing. The songs of the slave represent the sorrows, rather than the joys of his heart . . . Slaves sing more to make themselves happy, than to express their happiness." To make one's self happy, though, is a great gift, and when the ability to do so is shared with many others, there is the seed of good entertainment.

There were references to the music of the slaves that were not so positive. A Black writer in 1881 remarked on his race's "devotion and skill in the delightful art of music." However, he said more: "But the music of which I have been speaking was never cradled, so to say, in the lap of science; although its strangely fascinating sweetness, soulfulness, and perfect rhythm's flow, has often disarmed the scientific critic. It is a kind of natural music."

The same Black writer concluded: "Slave songs are valuable as an expression of the character and life of the race which is playing such a conspicuous part in our history. The wild, sad strains tell, as the sufferers themselves could, of crushed hopes, keen sorrow, and a dull, daily misery which covered them as hopelessly as the fog from the rice swamps . . . to breathe a trusting faith for the future . . . in Canaan's air and happy land, to which their eyes seemed constantly turned."

There is no need to look further for the intense feeling expressed by Black musicians today. It is not in the blood, it is in the soul. And if all music is a kind of soul "expressing," then the journey from West Africa, to the huts of slaves and all the years since, have left for Black musicians a powerful gift to at least partially balance the ordeal which created it.

Music and musicians change from generation to generation, with young enthusiasm and often with the disapproval of those who preceded. Rap, be-bop, and rock may be incomprehensible to elders but Black musicians have maintained the song of the soul. It has been a change of innovation, resistance, and the triumph of indomitability.

A free Black writer of the mid-19th century refers to the first introduction of choral singing into the A.M.E. Church in Philadelphia between 1841 and 1842. "It gave great offense to older members . . ." and they left and never returned. But the innovation of choral singing soon gained general acceptance, and the same writer said: "A choir, with instruments as an accompaniment, can be made a powerful and efficient auxiliary to the pulpit."

People have been heard to say: "I have no instinct for music." Few Blacks would make so sorrowful an admission. From freedom, to slavery, to freedom, to ongoing struggle, music has bared the soul of Blacks in America.

Chapter Two

Free
to
Bare the Soul

Chapter Two

Free to Bare the Soul

"Blues is the parent of all legitimate jazz"

W. C. Handy, (1873-1940) was the Father of the Blues. The Father he may have been, but he nevertheless said of the music he was reputed to have fathered: "Blues is one of the oldest forms of music in the world. It is folk music of the purest type. It represents the full racial expression of the Negro, and its distinguishing characteristics are throwbacks to Africa."

Blues are heavy, so heavy that some cry at the expression of the word. It has been said that "the blues is an honest expression of what one is going through." It is well to remember that Black musicians, throughout American history, have not only been going through a racial experience, but individual lives as well. W. C. Handy had his own experience.

In his earliest boyhood, Handy was fascinated by musical instruments and those who played them, and he set his heart on having one. "Setting my mind on a musical instrument was like falling in love." For a year, he saved every coin and in time he went to the store, pushed his coins up on the counter, and came home jubilantly with a guitar. At the sight of it, Handy's preacher-father bellowed that it was the devil and forced him to take it back.

Hit hard, but not defeated, he realized in steps that he must leave home if he was to make music his life. Everyone discouraged him, but he persisted and he learned vocal music in school, from a teacher who nevertheless condemned him for planning a career in music.

Of his decision to leave home, he later said: "Yes, music cheered me on, and played an accompaniment to many hard knocks." Later his father heard him play and said: "I am very proud of you and forgive you for becoming a musician." It is curious that some Black musicians have floundered in the face of opposition, while others flourished in a most supportive and friendly environment. W. C. Handy was one who bucked the tide and kept on going. There is a satisfaction to winning the game that does not look back on an easy road. Music was his support and perhaps he could have said, as Duke Ellington said a little later, "Music is my mistress."

After leaving home, Handy was offered a good job directing a white band in Michigan, and another job directing a Black band in Mississippi. He chose Mississippi, and, he said, the road that led inevitably to the blues.

W. C. Handy had something to offer, and he had the musicianship to make it appealing and attractive. And the blues was no less valid for having primitive origins. So much of life, after a coat of varnish, is still primitive. And it is often healthier to recognize this than to deny it. The blues are honest, and because it is up front with feeling, it has been able to reach, and allow, a soul that is often sorrowful. Handy saw the beauty of primitive music, and he saw for himself a livelihood.

He prospered. In a short time, he became a top bandleader in Memphis, where he wrote "Memphis Blues," and learned how to get it published. This first exposure to publishing was not without meaning for his future. "Memphis Blues" was a big hit. Not long after, at age 40, he wrote "St. Louis Blues," an even bigger hit, which we hear today, almost 70 years later.

"Jazz" was a new word at the time, and was felt and heard much more readily than it was defined. If blues was offered as the parent of jazz, then it is likely that jazz became dominant in time, so that blues became a part of jazz.

In 1918, Handy abandoned performing and went to New York City as a publisher. Things did not go well at first. A different man would have retreated. His eyesight failed, and his business was on the rocks. He wrestled with life and persevered. He was rewarded. His eyesight slowly returned. He was invited, on the strength of his compositions, to perform at Carnegie Hall, in a concert that was a clear success.

And then, Rudy Vallee recorded "St. Louis Blues" with the "Maine Stein Song" on the reverse side. The result was an international hit which gave Handy a broad and enduring reputation. Curiously, "St. Louis Blues" was written before "Memphis Blues" but its publication was delayed. Even more curiously, it was not original blues, but was based on a military march.

Publishing eventually became Handy's work, and he provided opportunities to Black composers in much the same way that Motown later existed to give opportunities to Black recording artists.

Earlier in this century, W. C. Handy was a household name, almost synonymous with musical expression. His progress from childhood owed a debt to difficulty. His success paid a debt to Handy himself, for his musical instincts and his willingness to assert them.

It is idle to wonder whether blues is jazz, or jazz is blues, or whether they are quite different. To say the least, they are congenial and it is time to take another step.

Chapter Three

All That Jazz

Chapter Three

All That Jazz

There are those who argue that jazz evolved in many place at roughly the same time; but, regardless, New Orleans is the sentimental favorite of this distinctive form. There was no doubt in the minds of the early New Orleans jazzmen that they were the creators. Willie G. "Bunk" Johnson was one of the first, and an immortal. In the late 1930s, he wrote as follows to two authors researching the beginnings of jazz:

Now here is the list about that Jazz playing. King Bolden and myself were the first men that began playing Jazz in the city of dear old New Orleans and his band had the whole of New Orleans real crazy and running wild behind it. Now that was all you could hear in New Orleans, that King Bolden's band, and I was with him and that was between 1895 and 1896 and they did not have dixieland Jazz bands in those days . . .

Bunk Johnson continued:

And here is the thing that made King Bolden band be the first band that played Jazz. It was because it couldn't read at all. I could fake like 500 myself; so you tell them that Bunk and

23

King Bolden's Band was the first one that started Jazz in the city or anyplace else. And now you are able to go ahead with your book.

This disarming certainty about the origins of jazz may have been a little self-serving, but it is a valuable account of events in New Orleans, whether or not it was first there, or was born in other places at about the same time. The description of the advantages of musical illiteracy appears often in the literature; so much so that in combination with common sense, it must be accepted as valid. Faking it "like 500," becomes a synonym for originality. The fences of conventional music were simply not there.

Jazz was born because it was time. At an earlier time, it might never have caught on. New Orleans caught the fever.

Very early in its newness, New Orleans jazz focused uniquely on funeral parades. With a slow pausing tread, the procession moved to the graveyard. Then it is recorded, "Once the body was interred, the mourning got over quick. About three blocks from the graveyard, the band would cut loose . . ." The response was joyous and infectious, and so typical of the Black musician's ability to draw from grief a feeling of happiness. Children danced along behind the free-spirited band, and adults left the curb to march in the procession. The saints came marching in. If the deceased was "over Jordan," then the living celebrated their life on earth.

Jazz scattered north with the Mississippi river boats, and Black migrations northward also made jazz popular beyond New Orleans. The almost immediate popularity of jazz in many places, and among Blacks and whites, was nothing less than a phenomenon. And the phenomenon provided an outlet and an opportunity for many Black musicians, individually and as part of the bands that were formed. As far back as 1850, it had been said of the early Black bands: "Sometimes a single Black fiddler answers the purpose, but on Saturday nights the music turns out strong, and the house entertains, in addition, a trumpet and a bass drum." For the bands of the turn of the century, it was Saturday night and far beyond.

The migration of music and musicians was geographical, but it was also something of the spirit. Jazz could have moved out of New Orleans without finding a home elsewhere. In fact, it was welcomed. In a relatively short time, the radio and the phonograph would take it where the musicians themselves did not go.

For many of the musicians themselves, there was a circuit, from New Orleans to Chicago to New York, and sometimes back to Chicago and even to New Orleans.

As jazz became more popular and appreciated, many people discussed what it *was*. Some said it was undefinable. Some said that it was "freedom of musical expression." Still others, including devotees, debated whether it was music: "Music is reading the notes you play. That is not jazz."

But jazz is surely music. It is the application of a style to music. Almost any music can be played in jazz style, and music can be created which is jazz from the start. There may be some truth to the statement that if you need a definition of jazz, you do not understand it. It's better to listen.

Definable or not, by 1917 Black musicians had spread jazz throughout the South, and north to Kansas City, Chicago and New York. There seems no doubt that New Orleans was the seed bed, and Bunk Johnson and King "Buddy" Bolden were undoubtedly pioneers. As proof of the informality of jazz, this statement was made of Bunk Johnson: "If you put down what Bunk had played he would say 'do you think I'm a fool?'" It was all spontaneous, all by ear, with none of the inhibitions imposed by notes on paper. To this extent, it was not music.

But as a vocal or instrumental rendition of the spirit, it surely is music.

The proof that jazz is music can be seen in the fact that jazz combos have performed with string quartet and symphony orchestras. Its key may be improvisation, which was a characteristic of African music. Jazz may be a case in which any attempt to formalize it will destroy its soul. This definition may illustrate: "Jazz is hot intonation and swing, generated by rhythmic accents and intervals. And a small interval of delay before attack."

It has been said that "without teacher, they went ahead on their own." But the early pioneers became teachers. King "Buddy" Bolden was one of the first. He was many things — a barber, a publisher, and the first great bandleader. And he was a cornetist without equal in his time. On a still night in New Orleans, Bolden's cornet could be heard for miles, from the river bank to Lake Ponchatrain. He became exhausted mentally and physically, and snapped during a Labor Day parade in 1907. He died in a State Hospital in 1931, known only as a barber. It was for later generations to know that his haunting cornet filled the night air.

Bunk Johnson succeeded Bolden as cornet king. He said of himself: "For faking and playing by head, I was hard to beat." Improvise he did, so much so that a bandleader smacked the cornet out of his mouth when he played the "wrong" notes.

Bunk Johnson was a musician himself, but perhaps he is best known for taking under his wing a young man named Louis Armstrong.

Louis Armstrong was one of those fortunates for whom bad luck became good luck. When he was 12, he discharged a firearm within the New Orleans city limits as part of a New Year's Eve celebration in 1913. He was arrested and sent to the Waif's Home, where the director saw musical talent in him and gave him a cornet. A brass band was formed at the Home, and it became well-known in New Orleans. At age 14, Louis Armstrong came out of the Home, and he knew how to play the cornet.

Bunk Johnson was Louis' idol, and he followed him in parades and on riverboat engagements. He went up and down the Mississippi on excursion steamers, linking up with bands and gaining experience as a performer. Asked about jazz by someone whose spirit was not sympatico, he said: "There's some folks that if they don't know, you can't tell 'em."

Although the best of the new music originated in New Orleans, many of the best Black musicians left the city for better opportunities. Sometime in the early 1920s, Louis Armstrong left New Orleans for Chicago, where, months before he arrived, he was already a legend. He quickly joined the band of Joe "King" Oliver, where his cornet became unique.

"Unique" was the word for Louis Armstrong throughout his long career. Personality had much to do with this, but so did endurance, physique, lung power, lip control and throat relaxation. He was never content to remain even "the best." He practiced during intermissions, and never rested in the search for improvement and innovation. He was a vital human being who liked to entertain.

In 1924, he was off to New York. But he joined a big band and was lost there. He lost his individuality and his uniqueness was stifled. He couldn't, as he said, "stretch out." But he did not consider his New York experience a waste. There were recording opportunities, and he made the most of them. His ability to see the positive aspects of an experience, which others considered a failure, was a valuable contribution to the years which followed.

He left New York in 1925 and returned — not to New Orleans — but to Chicago. He played at clubs and theaters, where people came just to hear him play and then left before the movie. It was during the second stay in Chicago that Louis added singing and a little acting to his performance. The crowds which heard him were in an uproar. He communicated the feeling that it was all right to relax, but at the same time, every performance was a stimulus. The word "unique" cannot be improved upon.

In 1927, at the Sunset Theater, his name first went up in lights. Two theaters were on respective corners of the same intersection and bands competed for patrons and sheer artistic sensation. Louis played at the Vendome Theater in the afternoon and the evening, and then rushed over to the Sunset, where he played until dawn. His energy was enormous, and his fame was rising rapidly. White and Black musicians flocked to hear him, but he had no imitators. Driven to excellence, he regarded rest as a necessary interference in his performances and practice.

In the spring of 1929, he went back to New York, and to true success. He was a star in his own right, and no longer under the wing of Joe "King" Oliver, who both nurtured and suppressed him. In later years, Oliver's life took a course quite different from that of Louis Armstrong. After 20 years in New Orleans, and 10 years as "King" of Chicago jazz, Oliver made a disastrous decision. In 1929, he turned down the job as bandleader at the new Cotton Club in Harlem. Duke Ellington took the job and made his reputation there.

In 1931, Oliver went on the road and never got back to New York, Chicago or New Orleans. By 1936, he found himself in Savannah. He sold vegetables and swept out a pool parlor. He died there in 1938 at the age of 53. He was buried in New York City in an unmarked grave.

Oliver was one of those who could help everyone but himself. He was hampered by stubbornness, temper, and bad timing. In 1922, he gave Louis Armstrong his start. In 1937, Louis played in Savannah and tried to help Oliver financially. He did not take the opportunity. As Louis said: "He didn't have no business sense."

A stunning success, and a sad failure. Louis Armstrong went on to decades of fame. The teacher was totally eclipsed by the pupil. Joe Oliver was a classic player. His tone was even and strong. He was always a little beyond the beat and he never wasted a note. He missed the good chances, but he never quite quit. From Savannah, he wrote a niece the following: "I don't feel downhearted. I still feel like I will snap out of this rut someday."

Louis Armstrong, the pupil who surpassed, died in 1971, more than three decades after his teacher. He performed until nearly the end, truly perpetuating the image of gregarious music and fun. Eileen Southern, an outstanding student of Black American music, said of him in 1983: "He was the first great jazz soloist. Over the long years, his genius remained immune to the onslaught of commercialism and to the ascendancy of other popular music styles. His reputation became worldwide."

We have visited with pillars of blues and jazz. We will make more visits. But we will look first at yet another kind of music in which Black musicians have excelled. It is fondly and happily remembered, but by fewer and fewer.

Chapter Four

Come On and Hear

Chapter Four

Come On and Hear

It has been said: "There has been ragtime music in America ever since the Negro race has been here." If that is true, we should logically look to Africa for the origins of ragtime. This has never been clearly demonstrated, but the link is strongly indicated. Regardless of where it began, its popularity was delayed until the late 19th Century. It was a late-comer upon the scene of Black music in America, and proved to be a form of music which white composers and performers readily mingled with.

Unlike jazz, which was generally contemporary with ragtime, ragtime was a composed music. In this fact may lie the reasons for its failure to endure the way jazz has endured. Composition inhibits the spontaneity, innovation, and creativity which the freedom of jazz encourages. Still, ragtime had an influence on jazz, and probably very early.

Scott Joplin (1868-1917) was the King of Ragtime. Born in Texas, of former slaves, his talent for music was apparent by age seven. He taught himself to play the piano and became an itinerant musician, playing in cafes and honky tonks. His earnings were slim, but he learned the music of the Blacks of the Mississippi Valley.

Ragtime became a craze during the 1890s, a time when Joplin was playing in saloons and bawdy houses in St. Louis and other Missouri towns. In March of 1899, he published his Original Rags, which met with some success.

Later in the same year, John S. Stark, a white music publisher, heard Joplin play a piano rag at the Maple Leaf Club and bought the piece for $50, with all royalties to go to the composer. These royalties provided a modest income, as the "Maple Leaf Rag" was a great success. Stark and Joplin went on to publish many ragtime hits, and Joplin became a household word. He also wrote an opera and a folk ballet.

Despite these successes, this quiet, introverted man did not seem able to sustain success; nor could he adequately support his family.

Joplin had a dream. He wanted to produce an art music, acceptable to both the Black and white worlds, in a classical form. In 1909, he settled in New York City, where he put everything into the realization of his dream. His vehicle was a new opera, "Treemonisha." He had such faith in his own abilities and in the understanding of the public that he sought beyond all reason to promote the production of the opera.

When the normal avenues to the theater were closed, one after another, Joplin took an unusual step. With what little money he had, he rented a theater. Without orchestra, costumes, scenery or lighting, he presented "Treemonisha" to an audience of pathetically few patrons.

What drives a man to present the central work of his life under conditions that almost guarantee failure? "Treemonisha" did fail, of course. The scene (which contemporary accounts describe) is enough to bring tears.

We see a small audience gazing dimly at a stage peopled by actors and actresses in street clothes. Instead of an orchestra, we hear the composer desperately trying to compensate at the piano. "La Boheme" would have failed under such conditions.

The tragedy grew. Joplin had sacrificed everything to create "Treemonisha." With its failure, Joplin's spirit had gone. His fortunes declined to the point where his wife had to run their household as a brothel. There were long depressions and only sporadic work. Finally, his mind and physical coordination left him. He was placed in a mental institution, where he died on April 1, 1917. He was 49.

Scott Joplin was never recognized as a serious composer in his lifetime. But fate is uncertain and over 50 years after his death, fame came to him. In 1902, Joplin had written a piano rag entitled "The Entertainer." In 1973, this music was used as the theme for a popular movie, "The Sting." It sparked a ragtime craze and the republication of Joplin's music. A more bittersweet result was a successful Broadway production of "Treemonisha" in 1975. To top it all, he was awarded a posthumous Pulitzer Prize in 1976, together with popular and scholarly acclaim.

Success in his lifetime might have prevented the depression which led to his institutionalization and premature death. It did not come. There is something about his story that makes one reluctant to leave it. It may be that ragtime, which later returned as a craze, will not return again. It is sufficient that in the 1970s, Scott Joplin received his honors.

Chapter Five

More Pioneers

Chapter Five

More Pioneers

Three giants among early Black musicians have passed before us. They represent the blues, jazz, and ragtime. There were many others who were contemporary or near-contemporary and who nourished the ranks of Black musicians. Some are remembered now, while the memory of others has unfortunately grown dim. Some, even in their own time, were known to only a few.

In the pages that follow we will come to know not necessarily lesser lights, but rather those without whom the future could not have unfolded. The end of slavery gave momentum to Black musicians; and, for reasons not fully understood, the 1920s were a decade in which Black musicians raised a voice which has not been silenced since.

Before the 1920s, a Black musician could write a memorable song without receiving credit for it. James Bland (1854-1911) wrote "Carry Me Back, to Old Virginny," which in time became the Virginia State song. Only then did many people discover that it was not a Stephen Foster composition. Like Scott Joplin,

Bland's recognition was posthumous. He was a little too early for the renaissance in Black music, which began with the end of World War I.

To examine that renaissance, where shall we start among so many musicians? They can only represent the period; just as in later decades, the rising and setting of stars is a galaxy of Black musicians too prolific to complete.

So let us begin with a giant who is largely unheralded in the popular sense. His name was William Grant Still. He was born in Woodville, Mississippi, on May 11, 1895, and he lived to post some important firsts among Black musicians. His schooling in music was first class. He studied at the Oberlin and New England conservatories, and with master musicians in England. He made his living by playing the violin, cello, and oboe in orchestras. He also did jazz arrangements and compositions for the Paul Whiteman orchestra.

Still wrote much Black nationalist music and was the first Black to use blues and jazz in a symphonic work. He wrote prolifically in all forms. He wrote abundantly for radio groups and for film and TV soundtracks.

The performance of his Afro-American Symphony by the Rochester Orchestra, under Howard Hanson (in 1931), brought him real recognition. In 1935, the symphony was played at Carnegie Hall. Then it was performed hundreds of times at home and abroad.

Still became known as the Dean of Black Composers. Leopold Stokowski called him ". . . one of the very greatest living composers of the New World." He registered three outstanding firsts. He was the first Black American to compose a symphony (1931). He was the first Black to conduct an American symphony orchestra. His opera, "Troubled Island" (1938) was the first opera by a Black composer to be performed by a major company, the New York City Opera.

Jazz influenced most of his work, to the point where jazz, when performed as a classical work, calls for definition. Like written music, the early jazzmen rejected all attempts to state what jazz was. But Still's accomplishments lead us to inquire. Jazz may be best interpreted by the senses, but the mind also has a role to play.

Jazz came from somewhere. It did not simply appear. It is said that the blues breathed soul into jazz, and ragtime was the clay of its body.

What was the body in which the soul reposed? First, jazz is syncopated rhythm. Syncopation, in music, describes a shift of accent when a normally weak beat is stressed. It can provide entertaining surprise, in combination with the stimulation of rhythm.

Jazz also involves the simultaneous playing of individual melody lines by members of a group. It might be called "mixing," or felicitous combat. Another feature of jazz is the use of vocal techniques in instrumental music. Still did not employ this feature in his symphonic compositions, but it has been popular in other jazz arenas. Finally, and perhaps most important, is the interpreter's free introduction of special melodic features. If any one feature makes jazz distinctive, it is this one. To employ it symphonically, while maintaining a symphonic structure, is a tribute to Still and other Black musicians who have composed classically.

In a little more earthy fashion, it has been said: "The real nature of jazz is organic. Just as Louis Armstrong, growing out of the great New Orleans tradition, sounds a new style, Roy Eldrige stems from Louis, and Dizzy Gillespie from Eldrige. These are the great trumpet players over the years."

William Grant Still was an outstanding classical musician of the period. There were others, and they played classical music and many other kinds of music.

There are few common denominators of Black musicians. One is their African heritage. Another, for most, is their descent from slaves. Most came from humble origins. And a surprising number had their first exposure to music in church, either singing, playing, or listening. Church music had a spontaneity that encouraged the release of feeling. It could, on signal, begin at any time during the service. Occasionally, the leader would give the signal, so as to terminate a preacher whose sermon had gone on long enough.

In the pages and chapters which follow, we shall not meet every Black musician, but we shall meet many who represent their profession and their race. Over the decades of the 20th Century, they have improved the quality of life for us all. Most of them are, or have been, well known. Omissions are unavoidable, in the sense that completeness is impossible. The absence of a favorite performer may be balanced by an introduction to someone who has been unfamiliar, up to this point.

Chapter Six

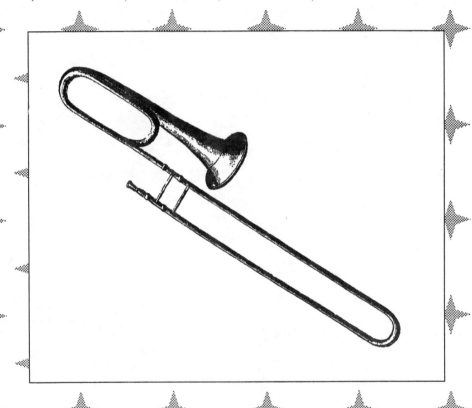

A Medley

Chapter Six

A Medley

The number of Blacks in the entertainment world is genuinely welcome. Even more encouraging is the number of Black female entertainers. A double barrier has fallen, and the discriminations of race and sex have become largely meaningless. In some areas, such as opera, Black women have been even more successful than Black men. In all other aspects of music, they have secured a strong equality.

So let us begin the chapter with a Black woman whose career has been exemplary, and a wonderfully successful voyage through decades of excellence.

Lena Horne was born on June 30, 1917, in Brooklyn, New York. Show business came to her early. In 1933, at age 16, she became a chorus girl at the Cotton Club. Cab Calloway was playing there, before an all-white clientele. She quickly became a featured singer, but her protective mother came to the Club every night to guard her virtue. This tended to isolate her from the rest of the cast, and retard her social development outside the Club.

Her schedule at the Cotton Club called for three shows a night, seven nights a week, plus appearances at obligatory political functions. She did all of this for $25 a week. Eventually, she left the Cotton Club for a singing job with the Noble Sissle band, a noted Black orchestra of the day.

In the Fall of 1946, when the Cotton Club had closed, she returned to New York to cement her position in show business. Her credentials were already impressive. She had been a featured singer at the Cotton Club, she had sung with a major Black orchestra, she had appeared twice on Broadway, and she had made a Hollywood film. Despite all this, she was insecure in New York, and her Mother's hovering had damaged her ability to live alone. She had difficult days and was unable to find a job. Eventually, Charlie Barnet's all-white band hired her as a singer and she got along very well in that setting. Recordings and night club appearances marked her as an outstanding blues singer.

She had returned to Hollywood in 1941, and the following year she signed a long-term film contract. Her career started slowly there, but in time she was the toast of the town. Some of her films included "Cabin in the Sky" (1943), "Stormy Weather" (1943), "As Thousands Cheer" (1944) and "Words and Music" (1948). She appeared in Broadway revues and on television. She made several European tours and was well received. She felt especially comfortable in Europe.

Lena Horne's Hollywood career was curtailed by her refusal to play roles which she felt were demeaning to Blacks. She stood her ground and paid the price, and in the long term, she still prospered. She was the nation's top Black entertainer. This happened despite the fact that she was smeared and black-listed in the Red Hysteria of the late 1940s and early 1950s.

A Medley

Throughout the 1950s, she was a major cabaret star. In 1967, at 50, she described herself as "just beginning to bloom." She appeared in Carnegie Hall, and was often heard on the radio.

In 1981, she opened on Broadway with "Lena Horne: the Lady and Her Music." She was a triumph, a one-woman sensation. Said one seasoned critic: "I guess I didn't know her at all."

Even today, Lena Horne makes an occasional, and scintillating, appearance on television. Young viewers are astonished when told that she is in her seventies.

Lena Horne, in her own words, is "a certified veteran of living." Her sophisticated bearing and sparkling personality have done much to change the unfair stereotype of Black entertainers. The trait that has characterized her to this day is professionalism. She still takes a vital delight in being alive, and is proud of what she's done. She should be. As an aside to her musical career, she has quietly contributed of her human and material resources to a spectrum of worthy causes.

Women, principally as singers, have been standouts in Black music. Few have had the sixty-year career of a Lena Horne, but we can reach back into the early years of the century, and find their marks on the present.

Female Black musicians had a double handicap — their race and their sex. It was 1920, for example, before the first Black woman was permitted to record a song. Mamie Smith recorded "Crazy Blues," which sold 100,000 copies in its first month. The Decade of the Classic Blues Singers was underway.

Ma Rainey is today acknowledged as "The Mother of the Blues," but when she passed away in 1939, the music world gave her almost no notice. It became common for a Black musician who wanted fame either to wait for 50 years after death, or to go to Europe. Ma Rainey had made her singing debut at age 14. She introduced the term "the blues" before it was widely used by way of W. C. Handy's "Memphis Blues." By 1917, she was playing the South with her own show. Like so many successful Black musicians, she did not read music.

Jazz historian Charles Edward Smith once wrote of Rainey: "She was the voice of the South, singing of the South to the South." Today Ma Rainey is a national treasure.

A famous contemporary of Ma Rainey was Bessie Smith. As a blues woman she was a mass hypnotist. Her work extended far beyond her day. Of the 180 songs she recorded for Columbia, 160 are still available!

Bessie Smith was performing for nickels and dimes at the age of 9. Her reputation quickly grew as she trained chorus dancers by day and sang at night. She was a deeply religious person, and her blues seemed almost to be hymns. At the end of the 1920s, she was a superstar. But in the early 1930s, the big money in the blues was over, for Bessie Smith, Ma Rainey and others. Bessie Smith died in a car accident in 1937.

Three singers are said to have pioneered American jazz singing; Ethel Waters, Louis Armstrong and Billie Holiday. Louis Armstrong we have met. Billie Holiday we will meet. Ethel Waters left us her autobiography and we will take advantage of it.

She wrote:

"My whole family could sing. There was no doctor or midwife. There was one emotional outlet my people always had when they had the blues. That was singing . . .

My family and the other families who lived in those alley homes harmonized without any instruments to accompany them. There were musicians in the neighborhood, fellows who played the banjo, mandolin, guitar and the bells. But they played at parties and sometimes on street corners. And we never had the money for a party."

That quotation is just as useful in describing the origins of Black music as a book of scholarship.

In 1917, Ethel Waters stole into a saloon Halloween party and sang. Two vaudeville listeners persuaded her mother to let them take her on the stage in Baltimore. At the time she said: "I couldn't see any bright future for myself in show business." But she seemed to have a sense for show business. They liked her in Baltimore. She got special permission to open with "St. Louis Blues," perhaps the greatest blues song of them all.

At the end of her act, she would take off her costume and makeup and rush out front to hear what people thought of her. They liked her and she kept going. Years later, she observed: "There was no radio then killing off popular songs in six weeks."

She was a trouper. At one performance, she was so sick that she was carried on stage and put in a chair where she sang and then fainted. That's a trouper.

She began to tour and record, and her tours sold her records. Of the band, when they played poorly, she had this to say: "I told them they sounded like Jenkins' band. This was the famous kid band sent out by a Charleston orphanage. That band has developed some first-rate musicians, but as kids they didn't toot any dream symphonies." Slowly but steadily, Ethel Waters spiraled upward to better bookings.

She observed: Talent can be developed, but no one in show business discovers it. Only the public can do that." So she sang to the public, on the road, in New York City, in theaters, and night clubs. She was a success, but it required a trip to Europe for eight months to confirm her success. While in

Europe, she had delicate throat operations which saved her voice.

Her singing of "Stormy Weather" proved a turning point in her life. It was "her song" and Irving Berlin came to the Cotton Club to hear her sing it. In 1934, she starred gloriously in Irving Berlin's "As Thousands Cheer." Much later, she starred with Lena Horne in the movie "Cabin in the Sky." She died in California in 1977.

Billie Holiday was the third of the great jazz pioneers. If her personal life was in some ways a song of the blues, her musical contributions survived, and survive today. She was born in 1915 in Baltimore, Maryland. Her given name at birth was Eleanor Fagan. In 1928, she moved with her mother to New York City, where she was inspired by the recordings of Louis Armstrong and Bessie Smith. At age 15, she began to sing professionally at a Harlem night club. In a very short time, she became the outstanding Black singer to emerge in the 1930s. She became known as "Lady Day," and gained international fame for her earthy blues style. Her recordings and her band engagements with Artie Shaw and Count Basie made her even more well-known, as did her cabaret appearances.

All through the 1940s and 1950s, she performed as a single. And then the blues came and got her. Her career declined after a narcotics arrest in 1947. She never disguised her vulnerability, and even sang about it. One of her last songs was: "Don't Weep for the Lady." In 1959, at age 44, she died in a New York hospital, under arrest.

Billie Holiday's is not the saddest success story on record; but is sad enough, considering the sensitivity with which she touched so many listeners. She gave so much in a short life. It does not destroy all of that to recognize that her mistakes were finally fatal. She is ranked among the top three singing influences in jazz, and at the mention of her name, that is the memory.

Mary Lou Williams, the pianist, was a giant of jazz. She began learning jazz piano at age three. Her mother, in the best jazz tradition, believed that formal study would ruin Mary Lou's ability to improvise, and so there were no piano lessons. Instead, she exposed her to musicians. She let her hear music, and she let her hear creativity. At age six, Mary Lou was going out on professional appearances and bringing home handkerchiefs filled with coins.

A six-year-old breadwinner would stand out in any society. A six-year-old who won the bread by playing jazz piano would very possibly find herself on television. Having started playing at age three, May Lou must have taken her six-year-old debut in stride. At an age when most children get their first allowance, she proudly brought home handkerchiefs full of coins to a needy family.

In 1930, Mary Lou Williams made her historic solo piano recording of "Night Life." She was unaware that she was being recorded, and her naturalness came through brilliantly. It was a hit, and is now a classic. She was active into the late 1970s and died in 1981.

Music is a bridge. It spans generations, styles, races, and even nations. The origins of American music are basically European and particularly German. The Afro-American transformation of this influence into something unique is a true experiment in folk music. It adapts and changes continuously, so that there *is* a bridge, if we look carefully, from Africa, and then from the slave songs, to Rap and house music.

Chapter Seven

The Aristocrat

Chapter Seven

The Aristocrat

Duke Ellington was born in Washington, DC, on April 29, 1899. He grew up listening to the piano and at the age of seven, he began lessons. He was a tolerable student, but in those years he was distracted by ball-playing and the other activities of young boys. He played at a church concert and was complimented, but he let it slip away. He did not return to music until high school. Along the way, at age eight, Edward Kennedy Ellington became "Duke."

He returned to music, but in high school he showed equal facility in art and drawing. He won an NAACP competition in art, but turned down a scholarship to the Pratt Institute of Applied Arts in New York City. Apparently he did not choose to commit himself at this point. Sometimes a career choice is better when one takes time to weigh the options.

A high school friend made a difference. Edna Thompson was a more disciplined musician and her friendship and interest made a deep impression on Duke Ellington. With her encouraging shoves, he went after the complexities of music with intensity. And he was remembered, even in those early days, as a creative musician. He was versatile. A ragtime band was formed in his high school and he quickly became its leader. With Edna's encouragement, his diligence increased and he began to practice two and three hours a night.

Ragtime was his favorite in these early years. He played piano for house parties and with bands. He said of those days: "I could never catch on to what anyone else played, so I developed my own stuff." His own stuff was so good that when he went into clubs and volunteered to play, he ran those ragtime stars "right out of the joint."

One night, when a drunken cafe pianist passed out on his stool, Ellington leaped forward and began playing his own composition, "The Soda Fountain Rag." "I was established," he said.

At this point, he left painting behind, and even left high school a few months before graduation, to pursue his music. It was 1917, and wartime Washington was very receptive to his novel music. He began to organize a band of real quality. He was most successful when he wasn't penned in by forms, when he was allowed room for creativity. If he was to do things, he had to be free to do them.

As his experience grew, Ellington began to make money. In 1918, he married Edna Thompson, whom he had known since grade school and who had done so much to urge him on in high school. In 1922, he went off to New York City with his fellow musicians and they became penniless and stranded. After finding $15 on the street, they returned to Washington.

In time, he went back to New York with his companions, and this time they were successful to the point where they were household names. They were described as "self-assured men of the fast world of 1923." They became synonymous with good jazz, and attracted such fans as Al Jolson and Jimmy Durante.

The Aristocrat

Duke Ellington, although no extremist, responded to neo-Africanism and the raised consciousness of American Blacks. Sounds of the jungle crept into his music and were evident thereafter. They were effective and audiences were responsive.

Ellington was one of the first jazz musicians to take advantage of the phonograph. Radio was also good to him, especially after he moved to the Cotton Club in late 1927. Theater appearances and recording sessions added to his schedule and the money was rolling in. Everything seemed to have the Ellington touch, from the sound of his remarkable band to one great soloist after another.

He was responsible for the first use of the word "swing" to mean "jazz." He recorded a song, "It Don't Mean a Thing If It Ain't Got That Swing." It was a big hit and represented a corner-stone of his musical credo. His band was always in tempo, always secure behind the drive of his rhythm section. He knew how to do it.

Louis Armstrong had been to England in 1932 and had not made a great impression. In 1933, the British awaited Duke Ellington with more interest. He was wildly received, with one sellout after another and rave reviews from the press. When he went to Scotland, he was preceded by criticisms that his music lacked form and was crude. In return, he made a comparison with the wild swirling of bagpipe music. They got the point.

From Britain, he went on to Paris. Fans came from all over Europe to hear him there. Of his European tour, Ellington said: "The main thing I got in Europe was spirit. It lifted me out of a bad groove. That kind of thing gives you courage to go on. If they think I'm that important, then maybe I have kinda said something . . ."

He had always resisted suggestions that he tour the South, resenting, as he did, the treatment of his race there. But when he returned from Europe, his feelings softened. And so in the autumn of 1933, he went to Texas. In Dallas, the crowds went wild and all theater attendance records were broken. Fort Worth was the same, and a year later in New Orleans, there were throngs to see him off.

In 1934, Ellington recorded "Solitude," his biggest hit to date. It was followed by "Moonglow." Swing was rapidly coming in to replace the old jazz, and there was much debate on just what swing was. Among countless definitions was that of Louis Armstrong, who said" "Swing is my idea of how a tune should go."

At first, Ellington hung back in embracing swing. He was still enormously popular, but he was a little left out of the growing ranks of swing. Then in 1937, he made an appearance on the CBS Saturday Night Swing Session. It put him on the swing map. The Chicago Examiner headlined: "Ellington Master of Swing Music." He said: "Swing is not a kind of music. It is that part of rhythm that causes a bouncing, buoyant, terpsichorean urge." In a 1938 *Life* magazine poll, Duke Ellington was one of the "Twenty Most Prominent Negroes in the United States."

At about the same time, there was a wonderful little occurrence at the Cotton Club. Ellington noticed a very dignified, white-haired gentleman come into the Club and take a table, listening to the music. Ellington recognized him as the great conductor Leopold Stokowski. Ellington greeted him and sat down. Stokowski asked him: "What are you striving for in your music?" Ellington replied: "I am endeavoring to establish unadulterated Negro melody, portraying the American Negro." Upon leaving, Stokowski gave him two tickets to the next night's concert at Carnegie Hall. Poles apart musically, the two celebrities had conversed and shared in harmony. And that's what harmony is.

In 1939, with war clouds gathering, Ellington made a second trip to Europe. In Stockholm, on April 29, he had his 40th birthday and a very warm outpouring of flowers and good wishes. Returning home, he had even more success. This often happened when Black musicians returned from European tours. The attitude at home seems to have been: "Gee, they must be pretty good."

A composer named Billy Strayhorn began to contribute many top songs to the Ellington band. Strayhorn was riding the New York City subway and was composing a tune as he rode. He spontaneously named it "Take the A-Train" and the association of the song with Duke Ellington is now legend. It was rapidly picked up by Glen Miller, Cab Calloway and others. It is still a classic and has been background for an Amtrak commercial on television, 50 years after its composition. Radio reports of his death played the song in the background.

On January 23, 1943, Ellington made the first of several appearances at Carnegie Hall. To mark the occasion, a plaque was presented to him, bearing the names of thirty-two musicians who congratulated him on his achievements. The plaque contained names ranging from Leopold Stokowski, Eugene Ormandy, Marian Anderson, and Cab Calloway to Artie Shaw.

The appearance of so many classical musicians' names on the plaque is intriguing in terms of who Duke Ellington was and how he was perceived. He was, in a way, a classical musician. Though the music of each was greatly different, Ellington and Stokowski were kindred souls, and each touched the life of the other.

The 1940s were premium years for Duke Ellington. He gave concerts at Carnegie Hall in 1943, 1944, 1946 and 1947. For years afterwards, he continued to appear on radio, TV and at many dances. Since his death in 1974, record companies have issued a steady flow of Ellington music never available during his lifetime. There are even studio sessions taped at Ellington's expense and added to what he called "the stockpile." Landmark musical occasions are now rediscovered and available. Other recordings (for example those in 1962), emerged lusty and full-blown in 1984.

It is so typical of Ellington's earned aristocracy that he preserved unpublished recordings with the surmise that they would be valuable after his death. His works are truly classics. And Duke Ellington was such a classic performer that "performer" doesn't seem to be the right word. He was musical royalty. There has always been something very special about him — perhaps an inaccessible "never again."

Chapter Eight

Talented Quartet

Chapter Eight

Talented Quartet

Fats Waller and Count Basie were born in 1904. Dizzy Gillespie was born in 1917. Charlie "Bird" Parker was born in 1920, and his life, all too short, was momentous. Any one of them, alone, would be a commanding figure in Black music. If we look at the four of them, the impact is almost overwhelming. These four were jazz. As we shall see, Dizzy Gillespie survives. On the morning this is written, he appeared on the "Today Show" to discuss his new album, "Symphony Sessions," recorded with a symphony orchestra. At 72, he is a remarkable performer and a remarkable innovator. Each member of the quartet is remarkable.

Fats Waller was born in New York City, where the atmosphere of show business affected him early. He did not have to move there. Stars were born in many places, large and small. But sooner or later they had to be tested in New York City. Fats Waller had the good fortune to be born there.

He started playing the piano at age six, another in a string of early starters. At age fifteen, he was playing at the Lincoln

Theater in Harlem for $23 a week. That seems a small sum today, but for a teenager in 1919, it was a significant income. By the early 1920s, he had given Count Basie pointers on the organ.

For a time, he worked in Chicago with Louis Armstrong and Earl "Fatha" Hines. By 1938, he was probably as well-known as Louis Armstrong. He and Louis tried to work together, but their styles were out of synch. They were friends, and admired each other. But Fat's piano and Louis' trumpet did not make a kind of music that either liked. They gave up the attempt.

Fats had a habit of writing surefire hits and then selling the rights for a paltry sum. Carelessness cost him many thousands of dollars, and others capitalized on his talent. There is something attractive about not going after the last dollar, but greater self-interest might have been personally beneficial.

Through the late 1930s and early 1940s, Fats spent most of his time recording and traveling with his own band. He never cared for the road. He found it physically draining, and like many a Black musician, he did not look forward to the racial penalties which made a vexing chore out of such simple things as eating and sleeping. He expressed amazement that white audiences would cheer their heads off at his performances and then send him across the tracks to sleep. Of course, this was a problem common to many and discouraged some from going on tour, or in many cases, dictated where they would tour.

Fats was an infectious and uncontrollable comic. His music made him popular but his personality made him more so. He even made huge fun of his alcoholism, which ate away at his life. But before he died, he had a reputation as an excellent pianist and singer. By the early 1940s, he was successful in every way; but he never stopped casting about. Was he comedian, bandleader, song writer, or jazz musician? He wondered, even while it was quite all right to be all four. The story of his life ends with the statement: "He shed light and joy and kindness about him wherever he went." Few have earned such praise.

Count Basie was born in Red Bank, New Jersey on August 21, 1904. Red Bank is not far from New York City. His mother, sorely pressed financially, gave him the tuition for his first piano lessons. In the beginning, he wanted to be a drummer, but Fats Waller became his idol and the piano became his instrument. He learned his jazz piano technique and Fats also introduced him to the pipe organ.

New York City was full of opportunities to earn money at the piano. There were cabarets, saloons, theaters, dance halls, and rent parties. Rent parties originated in the South, and involved a party at the home of someone whose rent was due. There was entertainment, and everyone who came made some contribution to the payment of the rent. They were wonderful social events and served a very practical purpose.

Count Basie sometimes took Fats Waller's place in a touring show and traveled hundreds of miles on the circuit. Once, his touring company became broke in Kansas City and Basie was stranded, like others before and after. His resourcefulness was tested, but he struggled back to self-sufficiency by playing the piano in a silent cinema. Eventually, he joined more established groups in Kansas City and the experience he gained there, in the early 1930s, formed the basis of the later "Count Basie Orchestra."

Count Basie was not the first trouper to be stranded on the road. And he was one of those whose determination and talent could not be defeated. In playing piano for silent movies, he kept active musically, and bought some time in which to move on to something better. All the while he banked experience for the future.

In the summer of 1935, he formed his own group. At first, it was a different life. The bookings were arduous and the pay was poor. Later he said simply: "But we were all young then." Nostalgia for the lean years is common and has been celebrated in song. But how well Count Basie summed it all up. One can walk into a successful business and see the first dollar earned, framed on the wall. Some few succeed without struggle, but it may be that they miss the best part. Count Basie was "young then," a memory to be treasured.

The coming of radio was a great boon to music and musicians, and Count Basie was no exception. His group was heard even on experimental radio. One night (in a broadcast from Kansas City) they were heard by a man in Chicago — a man who was very influential in the world of jazz. The event was called "the most momentous chance audition in jazz history." Contracts and recording sessions followed in abundance. The impact of chance is a factor in any life. In this case an infant technology brought Count Basie to the attention of someone who could and did make a decisive difference in his career. By 1938, Count Basie's band was nationally famous, and along the way, a radio announcer had dubbed him "the Count." It became a time of extended bookings, over six months, and even a year, and he and his band found a kind of stability they had never known before.

The years of World War II were very active, with Basie riding a crest of popularity which swept him on into the 1950s. In addition, he was also composing some fine tunes, including the very popular "One O'Clock Jump."

The early 1950s saw a turnover in Basie's band personnel. There was a new band and a new sound. It was a big band, to replace the small group which had been called "an incubation of jazz." In March, 1954, the band made its first trip to Europe, playing mainly in Britain, to appreciative audiences. He began to receive honors from every direction.

Talented Quartet

The 1960s brought success in films and TV, and included a triumphal tour of Japan, an audience that had not been frequently entertained by American performers.

In the 1970s, he basked in a successful career, with cruises on the Queen Elizabeth II and in the Caribbean. In his last years he struggled against a heart attack, pneumonia, and arthritis.

He continued his musical life into the 1980s, to the last ounce. When he went to Britain for the last time, in September, 1982, he came riding on stage in a motorized wheelchair with a special hooter to announce his arrival. Like so many others, he was a trouper. He was the last of the great piano-playing bandleaders, and outlived Duke Ellington, Earl "Fatha" Hines and many others. He was willing to do the things that success demands, and he had some good fortune. His life spanned 80 years, from 1904 to 1984. He was musically active for most of that time and displayed that essential ingredient for progress — adaptability. After years of familiarity with one style of music, he wasn't afraid to build a new band, a new sound. Jazz is now under criticism for clinging to old ways. A look in the direction of Count Basie might be useful.

Dizzy Gillespie and Louis Armstrong are in a separate class as influential jazz trumpeters, with Dizzy earning fame as the "King of Bop."

Dizzy Gillespie was born John Birks Gillespie in Cheraw, South Carolina, on October 21, 1917, and seems to have adopted, early in life, a deliberately eccentric behavior. His father had a local band and stored the instruments around the house. When his father left the house, Dizzy would get out the instruments and experiment with each of them. An early exposure to so many musical instruments was an unusually rare opportunity.

When his father died in 1927, Dizzy won a scholarship to an industrial school in North Carolina where he could also study music theory and harmony. At age 14, he started on the trombone but quickly discovered that he didn't like it. He borrowed a friend's trumpet, and there began a lifetime marriage.

At eighteen, he found himself in Philadelphia, in a band that was a going concern. But his eccentricities worked against him, especially his comic routines and his excesses in dress. He was trying, through his horn, to unscramble a lot of things, but the other band members saw him as insane.

In 1940, Dizzy joined Cab Calloway's band and continued his reputation for the bizarre. He tried things so exciting and advanced that even he had not worked them out. Within the band, he was tolerated rather than applauded. He did not have it together, but he was trying ways that were revolutionary, if not sheer genius. He left Cab Calloway in September, 1941, after an altercation in which Calloway was cut. At the time, guns and knives were common self-defense items. The world of jazz could be wild and volatile and stir the emotions. The expression of these emotions in music sometimes spilled over into interpersonal feelings and violence. Even so, there was surprisingly little, considering the times.

After leaving Cab Calloway, Dizzy worked with Ella Fitzgerald and wrote music for Woody Herman and Jimmy Dorsey. His tendency to be lighthearted and even comical disguised true musicianship. So it was with Dizzy's new music, "Be-bop." Duke Ellington once warned Dizzy Gillespie against letting his music be labeled. But in the 1940s, his music was labeled and the label was "Be-bop." And the critics were savage. As a result, one of the true revolutions in the first half-century of jazz was seen as the work of a collection of eccentrics in berets and goatees, who shook hands in contortions and played wrong notes. The fact was that Gillespie built his work on the most solid theoretical base ever constructed by a modern jazz musician; perhaps equaled only by Duke Ellington.

Through all the criticism, Dizzy went on, undeterred. He would not compromise his music to attract the big crowds. He was content to preserve an art form for audiences whose appreciation was true. In time, however, the big crowds came and millions of people, including Europeans, were eager to hear him play.

Dizzy had always had an ambition to lead a big band. From 1946 to 1950, he fulfilled that ambition. Eventually, the quality of the band diluted and Dizzy made mistaken efforts to hold his audience. Some labeled it "Mickey Mouse Music." But when that big band was at its uncompromising best, it had no equal.

On Christmas night, 1948, at Carnegie Hall, Dizzy Gillespie reached a musical summit in terms of performance quality and audience response. But one observer said: "From then on, the funny hats took over . . ." and in 1950 the big band broke up. Dizzy returned to smaller groups, having realized his dream of having a big band.

At the request of the U.S. Department of State, in 1956, Dizzy took a band on international tour. He played goodwill concerts in the Middle East and Pakistan, and later in Latin America. The tours were enormously successful and a healthy tonic for Dizzy's own spirits. After 1958, he toured with some of the finest small groups in the annals of jazz. He has now toured frequently in Europe and Asia. Like many artists before and since, he has been enriched and vitalized through playing for foreign audiences.

Dizzy Gillespie has had a knack for the impromptu, even for the zany. It has offended a few, but it has enlivened and deepened his music for many others, and on many occasions, from jazz festivals to funerals, honors have showered on him. At 73, he recorded "Symphony Sessions," the first jazz album ever recorded with a full symphony orchestra.

It was once said of him: "The whole essence of a Gillespie solo is its cliff-hanging drama. . . . He is always taking you by surprise, always shocking you with a new thought." Music as thought may itself be an unusual drama. If so, it is not surprising that it is associated with Dizzy Gillespie.

Charlie "Bird" Parker was born in Kansas City in 1920, and at fifteen was already on the road with a band. Even while young and untutored, he was a jazz explorer with a fine sense of harmony as his compass. He could play the tenor sax so fast that he astonished veteran players. He eclipsed them.

Tragically, early in his career, he became addicted to alcohol and heroin. As a result, his reliability suffered and that cost him job after job. Despite all this, younger jazzmen grew to idolize him as the one, unique alto sax. But his performance and creativity depended upon his mental and physical condition at the time. His output was frequently at the mercy of his terrible addiction. He drank heavily to get through recording sessions. At one session, he collapsed and was taken to the State Hospital, an experience he later described as "relaxin' at Camarillo." But when he was free of the problem, his jazz was unsurpassed. He had a genius for spontaneously creating fresh and thoroughly original solos. He even translated "Relaxin' at Camarillo" into a jazz masterpiece. He played from his soul, and he played from his experience. He was very close, in spirit, to Dizzy Gillespie, and once referred to him as "the other half of my heartbeat." Unfortunately, Parker's life, given to so much personal excess, was not as stable, or nearly as long, as Gillespie's.

Parker's music had a sense of both urgency and soul, with the two so neatly balanced that the music was a unique contribution to jazz. Within the main traditions of jazz, he had many new things to say. His famous "Parker's Mood," recorded in 1948, was slow blues in which he revealed much of himself. It was said that he sounded like a younger brother of Louis Armstrong. The newer music of his short life seemed easy to understand.

Charlie Parker died on March 12, 1955, at the age of 34. His genius was simply too intense to contain, and he succumbed to cirrhosis of the liver and the long-term effects of his heroin addiction. In his last hours, he sought the support of an old friend. The friends he left behind are too many to estimate.

Charlie "Bird" Parker's life and death were tragedy and triumph. But it would be a great mistake to conclude that his afflictions characterized his profession. They were probably no more common than in any other profession or in the general population. His was a personal tragedy; but he lived as few others.

Chapter Nine

The Beat Goes On

Chapter Nine

The Beat Goes On

Jelly Roll Morton was a genius of jazz. He was the first true jazz composer, the first to write down his jazz arrangements in musical notations. His "Jelly Roll Blues" was the first published jazz arrangement in history. In this was success and perhaps the seed of failure. The early jazz musicians had reveled in their freedom and creativity, precisely because they could neither read music nor write it down. There was constant innovation and adaptive fun. It was probably inevitable that in time someone would compose jazz. Jelly Roll Morton was the first and he was considered a pioneer; but when something is gained, something is often lost.

Jelly Roll hustled all his life, and had so many vocations that they detracted from his music. Still, he considered himself to be the inventor of jazz and became very irate at suggestions that someone else had that credit. His best years were in Chicago in 1923-28, when he recorded with King Oliver.

Later he went to New York City, to find that a lightning shift in jazz had put him out of fashion. His music was ensemble music, and jazz had become a music of soloists like Louis Armstrong. Why did he not adapt? Duke Ellington's success lay, in part, in the ever-changing and developing nature of his music. Many other Black musicians kept up with the times. Jelly Roll Morton, when faced with sudden change, seemed to lose his grip. One factor may be that he pioneered in writing jazz down and for too long had been ahead of his time — until suddenly the times caught up with him. From the vantage point of the 1990s, it would seem an easy thing for him to have sponsored soloists in his band. Perhaps he tried. Where others succeeded, he failed precisely because he locked things into place. There is a time to preserve what is, and there is a time to move with the flow. By the mid-1930s, Jelly Roll Morton was generally finished as a musical attraction and ended up playing piano in a little second-floor club.

He loved music to his dying day, and played his blues, rags, and stomps out of pure pleasure. His many dubious enterprises never completely distracted him from his first love. He was able, remarkably, to overcome the inherent limitations of the piano as a jazz instrument. He died in Los Angeles on July 10, 1941. If he died believing that he had invented jazz, so be it. It's possible.

In late 1989, at the age of 81, Lionel Hampton completed a tour with his band through England, France, Italy, and other European countries. On his return, he had a successful recording session, promoted his autobiography across the country, and is dickering for a movie deal. He is a remarkable man.

He was born in Birmingham, Alabama. The family migrated north to Chicago in 1919. They quickly found that Prohibition offered opportunities, and owned two houses — a residence and distillery. Hampton's first musical experience was drumming on the whiskey barrels. His indulgent uncle later bought him drums and a xylophone. He remembers "we were really well-to-do." He became interested in the big bands, but found it very difficult "to get heavy into jazz in Chicago in those days." But his uncle was a friend of many jazz artists and Hampton met many of them at his uncle's parties. As a youngster, he met Earl "Fatha" Hines, Alberta Hunter, and Bessie Smith. They would drop in after hours to "jam until my grandmother put breakfast on the table."

By his second year in high school, Hampton was playing drums in a local teenage band, and when the leader moved to California to check out the growing music business there, Hampton soon followed him to Hollywood. His first recording, an old 78 rpm of "My Mammy's Blues," was made there.

In 1936, after some recording sessions which produced immediate hits ("Moonglow", "Dinah"), Benny Goodman offered Hampton a one-year contract at $550 a week. In 1936, that was big money. It was pioneering for both Hampton and Goodman, since in those days there was no such thing as an integrated orchestra. Goodman tried to solve the problem by creating an integrated quartet as a separate specialty act. When they first appeared *Downbeat* magazine noted that: "Predicted Race Riot Fades as Crowd Applauds Goodman Quartet." The new group was a sensation, even on a carefully planned swing through the South.

Soon he had his own band and has spent 60 years in the big band business. When asked what keeps him going, he replies: "It's the music, man! . . . I did some stuff on the vibes last night so wild it scared me." At 81.

To his special credit, Hampton is noted for his encouragement of young talent. This is a trait that is not always common in any walk of life. There are other examples in the music world, but when added to Hampton's other characteristics, it demands respect.

When few big bands are left on the scene, Lionel Hampton and his crew survive.

"And you know why?" he asks, "because I please the people. I play the music they can understand."

Of more modern forms, he says:

"Most of that's not music (rock and roll). Bad as this rap trash. Got no melody. People want two things in the music business — they want a melody they can recognize and they want a good strong beat . . . staying in touch with your audience is one of the most fundamental things of all."

From age 15 to age 81 is a long performance. Lionel Hampton has stayed in touch with his audience. He fills amphitheaters and stadiums. He has prospered in every way, while avoiding the pitfalls that have drawn others into tragedy. When he was a child, he would go coatless into the cold in an effort to get laryngitis, to sound like Louis Armstrong. The story of his career in music suggests that childhood excursion was one of his more serious flaws. He has followed all the musical styles through the decades, has adapted, and has remained secure with fundamentals. His energy, at his age, is astounding. It is a comfortable bridge. With Lionel Hampton still on the scene, we can feel more comfortable about past, present, and future.

Gospel music may seem a long way from the music of Lionel Hampton, but the spirit is common to both. They exist together as examples of distinctive black music and of artists who are contemporary and talented.

Thomas Dorsey, born in 1899, is called "The Father of Gospel Music." His father was an itinerant Baptist preacher who settled in Chicago about 1916. On a visit to Atlanta, Dorsey met the celebrated stars of vaudeville, and he himself became noted for his blues. In time, he also began to write religious music.

A preacher, not his father, ignited his desire to write gospel and may have been the first person to use the term "gospel song" to describe the church songs of Blacks. Dorsey sold and sang gospel, church to church. He organized a female trio to sing his songs, first as backup to himself, and later as an independent group. He was a tireless composer and organize of gospel singing. And he had a protege, who, more than any other person, was responsible for bringing gospel to the attention of the world. She was to say: "Gospel music is nothing but singing of good tidings — spreading the good news."

Mahalia Jackson was born in 1911. A choir singer at an early age, she was told by others: "You've got it." She had it. She eventually went to Chicago, where she became even more active in choir singing. All through the years, often on the revival circuit, she "plowed for the gospel." After 1945, she began to record. Success came slowly, but come it did. Eventually, some of her records sold a million copies, something unheard of for gospel music. She was "out of church."

She gave a gospel concert at Carnegie Hall and drew rave reviews from a media that had earlier not even bothered to cover gospel. During 1950, she toured the U.S. and Europe. When she arrived in New York for her second Carnegie Hall concert, she was the talk of the town, with TV appearances, interviews, and huge crowds.

By 1951, illness was threatening her career but she carried on. She made several movies with Pearl Bailey, Eartha Kitt, Ella Fitzgerald and Cab Calloway.

In 1957, her illness worsened and she became more and more fatigued. But still she went on. She appeared for Dwight Eisenhower, John F. Kennedy and Lyndon B. Johnson, and toured concert halls, stadiums, churches, prisons, and campuses.

Going abroad to London and India, she felt more and more the effects of her illness. She collapsed in Europe and died on January 27, 1972.

Both Thomas Dorsey and Mahalia Jackson came from religious roots that produced a kind of soft evangelism. Gospel goes on, with many fine singers, but these two were the pioneers. Gospel became well-rooted in the 1960s, when John F. Kennedy invited Mahalia Jackson to sing at his inaugural in 1961. She sang with sensitivity and depth for the largest audience she had ever held. Her 61 years and what she shared of them, are a reason for special "thanks."

Chapter Ten

A Classic Example

Chapter Ten

A Classic Example

Black musicians came to America bringing with them the music of their African tradition. Their music changed, often slowly, under the influence of a new environment. Popular Black music has retained, and even rejoiced in, vestiges of its heritage. And, of course, it is popular music to which most of us have the greatest exposure. Because of this, we may overlook some stunning successes of Black musicians in the area of classical music. We should not overlook them, because they represent their own special triumph, and because they point to a door that is open to others.

The first American Black classical musician may have been Chevalier de Saint-Georges (1739-99) who was born in Guadalupe of an African mother and the governor of the island. Chevalier trained on the violin in France and became a master. He wrote compositions of a high caliber. Another early Black classical musician was Louis Moreau Gottschalk, who was one of the first Black composers to win international renown. Both Chopin and Berlioz heard him play the piano and praised him highly. He was a violin prodigy at age 6, and later a brilliant concert pianist.

In modern times, Marian Anderson stands out as the pioneer Black artist in the world of classical music. She was born in Philadelphia on February 27, 1902. Like so many others, her first singing experience was in a church choir. But in no other way was she like so many others. She was soon singing professionally in Philadelphia and other cities. In 1925, in a contest sponsored by the New York Philharmonic, which attracted 300 entrants, she won first prize.

Beginning in 1933, her long European tours became triumphs. Arturo Toscanini heard her at Salzburg and told her: "A voice like yours is heard only once in a hundred years." She returned home to America, already a celebrity.

On December 10, 1935, a sensational appearance launched Marian Anderson on the greatest recital career of modern times. Within a short time, two recitals were scheduled in Carnegie Hall only weeks apart. She then embarked on a recital tour of the United States and abroad which would have staggered someone less strong. She gave 70 formal recitals in 1938, and 92 in 1939. She sang in Europe, South America, the USSR, Australia, the Middle East, and much of Asia. The world claimed her.

In 1939, history was made when the DAR barred her from singing in Washington's Constitution Hall. The furor which resulted went far beyond the world of music. She sang instead at the Lincoln Memorial before a throng of 75,000 with radio carrying the concert throughout the land. Four years later, in the midst of World War II, the DAR invited Marian Anderson to Constitution Hall. Earlier, in 1936, the Roosevelts had invited her to sing in the White House, the first Black ever to be so invited.

A Classic Example

In 1938, Marian Anderson received the first of 24 doctorates in Music. The honors were unprecedented and she responded by representing the best in America around the globe. She was part of the national treasury. In 1958, President Eisenhower appointed her as a member of the U.S. delegation to the United Nations. In 1954, she had opened the Metropolitan Opera Company to Black performers. The Met had been rigidly closed to Black singers since its founding. She had "the simplicity of the truly great."

On Easter Sunday, 1965, at the age of 63, Marian Anderson gave her farewell recital in Carnegie Hall. She chose a joyous program for a joyous occasion — Handel, Haydn, Schubert, Barber, Swanson, Britten, and a fine selection of Afro-American religious folk songs. Her voice was a thin thread compared to younger years, but the power to spellbind was still there.

Marian Anderson's magnificence was so special that she did credit to herself, her country, and everyone who heard her. A pioneer, in her situation, had to be truly great to push open the iron door and allow others to follow. She was as classical as the music she sang. Music is richer for her life and for memories her name invokes. Time after time, she handled fearsome "firsts" with calm and poise. Her grace under pressure reflected nothing but quality.

Black classical musicians have gained entry to concert halls as composers, conductors, singers, and instrumentalists. It has been more difficult for them, in some ways, because classical music had long been in place as a part of the white culture. Jazz, blues, spirituals, gospels, and other music forms were initiated by Blacks and were quickly and easily popularized. Nevertheless, the breakthrough into classical music has now been solidly achieved, and it stands as a fertile field of opportunity for aspiring Black musicians. A career in classical music may not be as lucrative as some other musical avenues, but it can be rewarding enough in both income and satisfaction.

An example of a talented Black classical musician was Howard Swanson, one of the most distinguished Black composers. He never received wide publicity, but he had something more — the respect and deep appreciation of other professional musicians.

He was born in Atlanta in 1907, and lived a long and productive life of 71 years. His mother was a pianist and a singer. He himself was a prize-winning soprano at the age of 6. His first real recognition came in 1950, when Marian Anderson sang one of his songs. The song was worthy, but it was typical of Marian Anderson, and some other Black artists, to give encouragement and assistance to other artists of their race.

In 1950, also, his "Short Symphony" was performed by the New York Philharmonic. It was voted the best work performed in the 1950-51 New York concert season. Swanson had originally planned to be a concert pianist, but his schedule left him little time for the long hours of practice, and he turned to composing instead. His output included songs, symphonies, concertos, chamber music, and sonatas. Many of these works have been performed by leading orchestras and artists around the world. In all of his music, there was a trace of the Black folksong, and echoes of the blues as a cornerstone of the Afro-American musical heritage. The style of his music was elegant, intense in its feelings and a powerful blend of sophistication and tenderness.

Howard Swanson is not a household word, but his music will continue to be played and enjoyed long after some popular music is forgotten. His recognition was delayed beyond the age when many a star has come and gone. He lived long enough to see his place in Black musicianship firmly established.

A Classic Example

Leontyne Price was born on February 20, 1927, and became an outstanding lyric soprano. In 1952, she undertook an international tour for the U.S. Department of State, and she proved herself an artist of superior quality. In 1961, she made her debut with the Metropolitan Opera, in "Il Trovatore." She received a 42-minute ovation, which ranks as one of the longest in the history of the Met. She also became the definitive "Aida" of her time. She was indebted to Marian Anderson for opening the doors of the Met to Blacks, seven years earlier. And so, it was fitting that on April 10, 1982, Leontyne Price stepped forward on the stage of Constitution Hall and opened the DAR convention with a concert honoring Marian Anderson. It had been 43 years since the DAR had barred Marian Anderson from singing in Constitution Hall.

Jessye Norman, born in Georgia in 1948, is a world-famous soprano at the peak of her career. She has worked in New York City and throughout Europe. She made her operatic debut in Germany in 1969. She was not received in her homeland until the 1980s. She debuted at the Met in 1984, and sang at the Reagan Inauguration. She pays tribute to trailblazers Marian Anderson and Leontyne Price.

Andre Watts did not have to wait long for recognition. He won prizes from childhood; and at age 16, he performed on national CBS radio. In 1963, he appeared at the piano with Leonard Bernstein and the New York Philharmonic, and he was immediately established as a prodigy. Now, in the early 1990s, he is a piano artist of international stature. At age 6, he made a wise choice in switching from violin to piano. Watts believes that there are great opportunities for Blacks in classical music. Of his own highly successful career, he says: "Part of me really has to genuflect inside when I mention names like Marian Anderson, William Warfield and Leontyne Price because I know the difficulty they had and I don't know how I would have fared if I had to put up with the same things." If they made it easier for Andre Watts, then Andre Watts has made it easier for yet another generation of Blacks in classical music. Present and future beckon.

It is not well-known that Coretta Scott-King, the widow of Martin Luther King, Jr., toured as a concert singer after graduating from college. She earned a Bachelor of Arts degree in Music from Antioch College in 1951, and a music degree from the New England Conservatory of Music in 1954. She made her debut as a concert soprano in 1958. She continued to tour widely, including a tour of India in 1959. She devoted time to Freedom Concerts and taught voice. In 1971, she received an honorary doctorate from the New England Conservatory. Successful though she was, Mrs. King sacrificed much of her career to the civil rights mission of her husband. Even so, she warrants inclusion as a distinguished Black musician.

Paul Robeson, born in 1898, was one of the greatest bass-baritones of American musical life. He won early fame at Rutgers University from 1915 to 1919 as a two-time All-American in football and graduated Phi Beta Kappa. Ironically, he failed to make the Rutgers Glee Club. He went to law school and practiced briefly, but his new bride urged him to a career on the stage. He had early success as an actor and a singer.

In 1959, he established himself as one of the great drawing cards of the musical world, by virtue of two sell-out recitals in Carnegie Hall, only five days apart. The next 15 years were very active at home and abroad. He devoted himself and his programs to the folk songs of his people and of the peoples of the world. Unfortunately, Robeson's views on Communism versus the American system made him unpopular with the United States government and people. He resided in the USSR for a time. Eventually, by the late 1950s, he was able to sing again in the United States and Europe, but after an illness in 1961, he never sang again. He died on January 23, 1976.

A Classic Example

William Warfield, another great Black baritone, made his debut on March 19, 1950. The critics reported "a phenomenal voice which he projected with complete artistry throughout a long and highly exacting program." The next winter he appeared in Washington as Porgy in "Porgy and Bess." His acting was as memorable as his deep-throated voice. By 1965, his recitals were so versatile that his program combined songs from "Show Boat" with "Four Serious Songs" by Brahms.

A critic has suggested that if William Warfield had been born in early times in Nuremberg, he would have been crowned as Meistersinger. It is easy to discover that since his father was a minister, he had early exposure to piano, organ, and voice. But the voice had to be there to flourish. He made a movie debut in "Show Boat" and also made major television appearances. From 1952 to 1959, he made five international tours for the U.S. Department of State.

Roland Hayes was the first Black singer to be accepted on the major concert stages of the United States. His pioneering appearances in late 1923 marked a dividing line in the history of Blacks in classical music. Five months later, Marian Anderson sang her initial recital on the same stage, and a year later Paul Robeson sang his first concert of spirituals.

Of Hayes, it was said: "Like so many other American singers, he found that the best way to build a career" was to leave for awhile. Acclaimed by English, French, and German critics as one of the great voices of the world, he returned to his own country, a true welcome, and a demand to hear him. In one season, he held 125 recitals. As late as his 75th birthday, on June 3, 1962, he was able to fill Carnegie Hall.

As people of the music world looked at Hayes' career in retrospect, one critic said that he had a radiance in him. "Call it soul perhaps." Another said of his last concert: "The white-haired figure on the platform embodied the aspirations, the innate goodness, the brotherhood of all mankind."

Anton Dvorak, the great Czech composer said this, in 1893, as he prepared for the premier of his New World Symphony: "In the Negro melodies of America, I discover all that is needed for a great and noble school of music." This is high praise, at a time when Black music in America had not gained the prominence that it has today. It is a recognition of a whole system of music which was born in Africa and refined in America. We have noted a few of the performers who were born and who became famous after Dvorak's observation. There are many others.

Leona Mitchell, born on October 13, 1949, became the first native Oklahoman to sing with the Metropolitan Opera Company. She had performed operatic soprano roles in college. In 1972, she debuted with the San Francisco Opera as Carmen. She sang with other operas and major symphony orchestras. In 1975, she played Bess in *Porgy and Bess*, and debuted with the Met as Micaela in *Carmen*. She toured Europe in a host of operatic roles.

Grace Bumbry, born in 1937 and an outstanding mezzo soprano, was the first Black performer to sing at the Wagner festival in Bayreuth, Germany. During the Kennedy administration, in 1962, she was called to the White House for a command performance.

Like so many before and after, her first exposure to music had been in a church choir. She won a national talent competition in 1954, and went on to universities. When she was named to play Venus in *Tannhauser*, in 1961, she was confronted with an outburst of hostility. She proceeded to win everyone over with her brilliance. Her big operatic voice was only moderately successful in Carnegie Hall, but overall, she is in a class with great Black singers.

A Classic Example

There are other well known Black singers and opera stars. They tend to be more women than men, but the doors remain open. Among composers and conductors, men tend to eclipse women. William Grant Still has already been noted as "the dean of Black composers."

There was another "Dean," Dean Dixon, born in 1915, and the first full-time Black American conductor of symphony music. He was born in Harlem, of West Indian parents. He organized an amateur orchestra in high school, which was so successful that many urged him on to a career in music. In 1941, at age 26, he became the first Black, and the youngest American, ever to conduct the New York Philharmonic Orchestra. All of this success had been nurtured by his parents who, among other things, took him on regular childhood trips to Carnegie Hall. Later, he went on to the Juilliard School and Columbia University. In the early 1940s, he was signed to conduct the NBC Summer Symphony and in 1975, he became director of the Frankfurt Orchestra in Frankfurt, Germany.

Florence Price (1888-1953) was the first Black woman to achieve distinction as a composer. She began composing as a child, and her lifetime output was prolific — symphonies, concertos, overtures, chamber music, and arrangements of spiritual and folk songs. In addition to serious composition, she wrote radio commercials.

Michael Morgan is currently (1990) assistant conductor of the Chicago Symphony Orchestra. At 31, he is one of the youngest maestros of any major orchestra. In 1980, he won the Stokowski Prize in an international competition in Vienna, Austria.

Other Black conductors are making names for themselves. James DePriest is music director of the Oregon Symphony. He won an international conducting competition in 1964, and worked with Leonard Bernstein. His work in Oregon has received national praise. The numbers are on the increase and include Kay George Roberts, music director of orchestras in Massachusetts — who has the added distinction of being a woman.

Another vehicle for Black musicians is the chorus. The chorus is especially appealing, because it can provide many amateurs with an exposure to disciplined and enjoyable music, and stimulate some to go on.

Black choruses began to appear in the 1920s. Hall Johnson and Eva Jessye were among the pioneers. Johnson, born in 1888, was well educated and trained and believed strongly in preserving the integrity of the spiritual. The Hall Johnson Chorus made its debut in 1928. Critics and the public were warm in their praise, and the choir was in demand for concerts, theater, and radio. In 1951, the choir made a long and successful tour of Europe.

Eva Jessye, born in 1895, was a pioneer woman choral director. She began her musical career as a teacher. In New York City, she formed a choir which was soon singing on radio in the United States and London.

College and university choruses and glee clubs have been very prominent. The Fisk University Chorus was especially well known, and toured the country giving fundraising concerts for the school. In the mid 19th Century, 7 years of touring by the Fisk Jubilee Singers brought $150,000 to the university. This was an enormous sum at the time. The alma mater of Martin Luther King, Jr., Morehouse College, has recently been in the news for the excellence of its Glee Club, ninety-eight strong. The thirty-year old director, David Morrow, has helped to establish the club as among the finest choral groups in the country.

A Classic Example

Seventy-nine years old, the Morehouse Glee Club has serenaded presidents, sung on countless soundtracks, and comforted mourners at times of national crisis. One member, while in high school, saw the club perform and commented: "I had never seen so many well-disciplined black men in uniform, outside the Marine Corps." Morehouse was founded in 1867, in the basement of a Baptist church. Like Black classical musicians, it has come a long way. Its Glee Club was chosen in 1969 as one of only three groups to participate in the International Choral Festival at Lincoln Center. In 1972, the U.S. Department of State sent the club on a cultural tour of Africa. Since then, it has been omnipresent at national, international, and regional functions.

There is so much that is fine in the past and present of Black classical music. Every name in this chapter is special, and there are many, many others. Those that appear are representative of a successful effort to enter into an area of musical artistry not originally open to them. And those who succeeded first did not turn their backs on those who struggled behind. Marian Anderson established a scholarship fund for young black singers. Roland Hayes often lowered his fees so that the poor of his race could hear him sing. And many established Black performers worked hard to bring young Black musicians to the attention of the public.

It is encouraging that Black classical musicians, despite a difficult road, have now gained entry at every level. It is also encouraging that those who have been successful have been very active in promoting opportunities for younger aspirants. The hard work of gaining entry has been done. Individuals may yet have a hard road, but Blacks are now solidly in classical music. True, it lacks the broad and incessant popularity among the young, that is enjoyed by other modern music forms; but it is a firm and enduring opportunity for those who have the inclination.

It may have seemed unusual to find the chapter on "Blacks in Classical Music," in the midst of chapters on better-known Black Musicians. But it points up the fact that classical music is very much a part of the Black musical experience, and need not be relegated to the status of a postscript. The blending is enhanced if we consider that elements of jazz have found a place in Black classical music. William Grant Still relied on jazz in his symphonies. Duke Ellington was in many respects a classicist who could converse on equal terms with Leopold Stokowski. Paul Robeson spent much of his career singing the folk songs of his people. Opportunity may lie in both directions. But in any event, classical music can be a fruitful choice, not only for performing, but for those listening to talented Black artists.

Chapter Eleven

More Excellence

Chapter Eleven

More Excellence

Duke Ellington once said: "Music is my mistress." Miles Davis said: "It comes before everything."

Miles Davis was born in Alton, Illinois in 1928. He was born of affluent parents, a circumstance which was rare among Black jazzmen. On his thirteenth birthday, he received a trumpet, and he was launched.

In 1945, he was sent to study at Juilliard in New York City. When he heard Billy Eckstine's famous band, featuring Dizzy Gillespie on trumpet and Charlie Parker on saxophone, he made up his mind to be a musician. He more or less apprenticed himself to Parker and received a musical education not available at any school.

As Parker's drug habit grew worse, Miles gradually drifted away from him and began his own lifelong experiment with music. He pioneered the "Birth of the Cool" and the cool jazz era. In the mid-1950s he put together a truly remarkable jazz group, including Cannonball Adderley and John Coltrane. The music was sensitive, understated, and lyrical. The group made historic recordings and toured the U.S. and Europe. Some of Davis's solos were called "imperishable" and among the most enduring statements in music.

In the 1960s, Davis assembled another collection of budding stars. They took jazz in a new direction, first using electric instruments and then blending in other music styles. As the 1970s began, Miles Davis was moving steadily toward rock.

Serious auto accident injuries kept him idle during most of the 1970s, and Davis organized a new band in the early 1980s. It was basically a rock group, although it sometimes included interesting jazz. Davis now has his critics, who call the music regressive. They long for the "gloriously adult music" made by Davis in earlier times and lament his more recent excursions into pop and rock. But he is still striking out in new directions, incorporating new instruments and sounds from the Caribbean, Africa, and elsewhere. He became quite taken with the music of Prince, in the late 1980s. He said: "Prince is from the school of James Brown, and I love James Brown because of all the great rhythms he plays."

Miles Davis is now in his early 60s, and recently said: "I like playing with young musicians. I want to keep creating, changing. Music isn't about standing still and becoming safe." His advice is good in many areas of life. Music and musicians have never progressed by playing it safe. Miles Davis has been especially innovative in pushing forward the frontiers.

There have been few Black musicians as distinctive as Miles Davis, but there have been outstanding ones of the same general era. One was Clark Terry, whose career as a trumpeter has included important associations with Duke Ellington and Count Basie. He also had some of the dazzling techniques of Dizzy Gillespie. Through all of these influences, he developed a unique and instantly recognized solo style. He was a mainstay soloist with Duke Ellington throughout the 1950s, toured Europe in 1959, and then spent twelve years with the NBC staff orchestra. In 1964, he had a surprising hit called "Mumbles," in which he vocalized the blues in a hilarious, incoherent fashion.

Terry is the inspiration behind the "Louis Armstrong Park" and statue nearing completion in New Orleans. Louis Armstrong is probably New Orleans' most famous son. Until Terry took up the task of a suitable memorial, Armstrong had never been permanently memorialized. The statue will be the centerpiece of an entire park.

Terry and Miles Davis were close friends. Terry was one of the few influences Davis would ever acknowledge. Terry was featured at the 70th birthday party of Duke Ellington at the White House in 1969.

John Coltrane was born in Hamlet, North Carolina in 1926. He learned the essentials of music from his father after moving to Philadelphia. He studied formally and informally in the jazz community there. He worked in the 1940s with the rhythm and blues band of singer and fellow saxophonist Eddie "Cleanhead" Vinson, and with one of Dizzy Gillespie's combos. In 1955, he was hired by Miles Davis to become the other horn in the most important small band of the decade.

He became a master saxophonist. By the time he left Davis in 1960, to form his own group, Coltrane was well-known, influential, and controversial. His fans hailed him as the liberator of jazz. He moved steadily away from the mainstream and into the "free jazz" movement of the 1960s. His own musical personality came to dominate countless established musicians. By 1965, he was a cult artist to young jazz aspirants and cult musicians. By the time of his death in 1967, Coltrane's music had become "impenetrable and puzzling." Asked for an interview a few years before he died, he declined and said simply: "It's all in the music."

Julian "Cannonball" Adderley was an almost mythical saxophonist, an expansive jazz soloist and one of the most popular members of the musical community. He was born in 1928, into a musical family in Tampa, Florida. He was an active jazz musician in his teens. He was a band director, and a leader of military jazz groups. Visiting New York in 1955, he dropped into a famous jazz club, played a few stunning numbers and became famous overnight. Almost immediately, he had a recording contract, and in 1957, he joined Miles Davis. In two years, he formed his own group and it became one of the most successful small groups of the 1960s and 1970s. Musically, he preserved the past even as he nudged toward the avant garde. He died after a massive stroke in 1975, at the age of forty-seven.

Bud Powell may have been the most important pianist in modern jazz. He was born in New York City in 1924, the son of a pianist father. He began playing at six, and until he was thirteen, he rigorously studied the classics. He encountered jazz in his teens and was drawn to Art Tatum, whose status among pianists was described by Fats Waller as "God." Powell dropped out of high school at fifteen, and went to work professionally. At Minton's in Harlem, Thelonius Monk introduced him to the world of jazz piano. By 1943, there were hints of a style that came to be known as be-bop.

Unfortunately, by 1945, Powell began suffering the mental illnesses that too often derailed his life and made his achievements inconsistent and sporadic. But George Shearing changed his style after hearing Powell play. That's a compliment.

Benny Goodman couldn't make up his mind about be-bop, but he could make up his mind about Wardell Gray. He said, in

1949, "If Wardell Gray plays bop, it's great." Gray made a hit with the big band and with the Benny Goodman sextet. Gray was a natural tenor saxophonist.

He was born in Oklahoma City in 1921, but he moved as a child to Detroit. In 1943, he joined the big band of Earl "Fatha" Hines. Moving to Los Angeles, Gray became one of the few bop musicians to stay clear of drugs. He played with Count Basie, in the 1940s and again in the 1950s.

In 1955, he joined a grand opening engagement in Las Vegas. Two days after the debut performance, his body was found in the Nevada desert, the neck broken. The circumstances were never discovered. Wardell Gray left his music, always fresh and new.

In the mid-1970s, a guitarist and singer named George Benson became a best-selling performer of pop with an album called "Breezin." Since then, he has become one of the best known pop music figures; one who has also demonstrated that he is a master jazz guitarist. Benson was born in Pittsburgh, Pennsylvania, in 1943. By the age of eight, he was earning money playing the ukulele. At age eleven, when he was learning the guitar, he recorded as a singer. He played in a rock and roll band. Then he heard recordings of Charlie Parker and Wes Montgomery, and jazz became his enduring interest. At eighteen, in the band of Jack McDuff, he first received the serious attention of the jazz world. Gradually, he began crossing over from mainstream jazz to mainstream pop.

Thelonius Monk is his own category of jazz. Until the late 1950s, Monk was generally talked down by his colleagues, long after the success of Charlie Parker, Dizzy Gillespie, and Bud Powell.

In the 1960s, after *Time Magazine* put him on the cover, there was a flurry of interest, mainly in his personal life but also in his music. Musicians who had written him off began to see that there was something much deeper than the surface peculiarities of style which had brought laughter.

Now, Dizzy Gillespie has praised Monk for his pioneering harmonic discoveries in the early be-bop days of the 1940s.

Monk's early life in music was not unlike that of many others. At six, he began teaching himself to play the piano. Formal lessons began at age twelve. By fourteen, he was playing rent parties and hearing many of the legendary Harlem pianists like James P. Johnson, who had a real influence on him.

In his teens, in the mid-1930s, Monk went on the road with an evangelist and became involved in incredible jam sessions in Kansas City. Mary Lou Williams recalled later that Monk, during these teenage days in Kansas City, had essentially developed the style that he worked in all his life.

Although Monk worked with the bop innovators of the 1940s, his own music was not welcomed as was bop. It wasn't until the 1960s, when John Coltrane put the stamp of approval on Monk, that other musicians accepted him.

Decline set in at the end of the 1960s. After mid-1976, Monk went into almost total seclusion, seeing no one, and speaking little. There may have been the persistent conviction that his music was unappreciated. He died after a stroke on February 17, 1982. Since that time, it has been a case of the music world catching up with Thelonius Monk.

A film was made in the 1960s, based on the life of Thelonius Monk, "*Thelonius Monk: Straight No Chaser.*" It is a documentary, shot for German television. A critic responded: "The best way to hear jazz is to see it." It is a film in which music has center stage and personal pathos is in the background. "For anyone who got to know Monk's music solely through recordings, as I did," says the critic, "seeing him perform is revelation." The film also inspired this comment: "Great jazz is a spontaneous drama of cooperation and competition, of playfulness and daring, of craftsmanship and serendipity. It's a drama of individuals trying to top themselves and of personalities working together." There are other, more musical definitions of jazz, but that one probes the essence.

For three decades, 1950-1980, Charles Mingus, as bassist, composer and leader, was one of the most powerful forces in jazz. He brought the bass into the center of the music, as a catalyst of continuous action. Like Duke Ellington, his music was involved with the blending of the traditional and the new.

In the late 1960s, Mingus was afflicted with poor health and was disgusted with the commercialization and complications of the jazz scene. By the end of the 1970s, he was conducting from a wheelchair. He died in 1979.

The tenor saxophone has stamped many a memorable Black musician. For example, in the early 1920s, Coleman Hawkins virtually reinvented the tenor sax and made it a jazz instrument. His style and tone were major influences for over thirty years. Lester Young was at first penalized for not playing like Coleman Hawkins, but then he himself became established as a hero of younger musicians. Budd Johnson, John Hardee, and Ike Aubec all made special contributions on the tenor saxophone. Ben Webster, somewhat older than many, had a special influence. A disciple of Coleman Hawkins, he generated his own disciples. He played with Bennie Moten, Fletcher Henderson, Cab Calloway and others. He was best known for his years with Duke Ellington.

Art Pepper, a leading alto saxophonist of his generation, shared with a few others the distinction of not being an imitator of Charlie Parker. Still, he absorbed some of Parker's be-bop styling, and incorporated some of John Coltrane. Since his death in 1982, at age 57, his music has become increasingly recognized for its power and appeal.

Bill Maceo played the most powerful piano in jazz, with no need of instrumental support. He could play boogie in all tempos, and he excelled as an accompanist to vocalists. He hit his peak in the mid-40s. He died of a stroke at age 48, on February 26, 1953.

This chapter on selected jazz artists cannot omit Hazel Scott and Eubie Blake. Hazel Scott, born on June 11, 1920, became a great jazz pianist and singer. She began playing the piano at age five. Her mother was an orchestra leader, and Hazel joined early. She first appeared as a jazz soloist in 1935, with Count Basie. By 1936, she had her own radio series. In the 1940s, she was a leading pianist-singer, anchored in New York nightclubs. She worked in Broadway musicals, Hollywood, and on her own television show. She spent the better part of the 1960s in Paris and Switzerland; and she died not long after her return to the United States. She was popular because of the vitality of her talent.

Finally, in this sequence, let us note Eubie Blake, the "Grand Old Man" of jazz pianists, who played on television and at festivals, into his 99th year.

Chapter Twelve

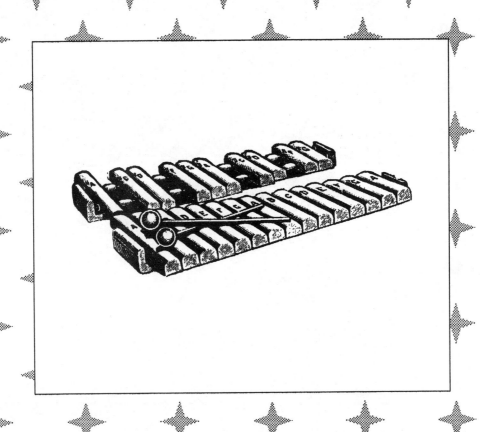

Moving on in Micro

Chapter Twelve

Moving on in Micro

The more we advance in time, the more we are in awe at the outpouring of Black music and the numbers of worthy and outstanding Black musicians. We are driven to be selective. In general, the focus will deal with the period from the 1940s to the present and will survey Blacks of all artistry, across many musical forms and styles.

Ella Fitzgerald spans almost the entire period. She has been a superb interpreter of popular songs, integrating elements of jazz, blues, and soul. In 1934, a frightened sixteen-year old, she entered a talent contest at the Harlem Opera House. She had planned to dance, but her knees shook so that she couldn't. Without hesitation, she said: "I'll sing!" And that quick decision changed her life. She was spotted by Chick Webb, the noted drummer and bandleader; and she became his featured vocalist. In time, she was touring the world with Duke Ellington, Dizzy Gillespie, and others. Duke Ellington enjoyed working with Ella. He even recorded an album of his own, in four movements, entitled "Portrait of Ella Fitzgerald."

Through the 1950s and the 1960s, her popularity and her workload increased, with recordings, concerts, and touring. The English called her the Maria Callas of the blues. In March of 1965, at age 47, in Munich, she suddenly lost control in the middle of her performance. She faltered, stopped singing, and was led from the stage. She later regained her composure and finished her performance, but it was a warning to slow down. However, on the contrary, work seemed to help her, and she kept on going.

The death of Louis Armstrong on July 6, 1971, deeply affected Ella, not only because of who he was but because of what he represented in music and among Black Musicians.

In 1982, Ella's twelfth Grammy Award came her way for an album done with Nelson Riddle. The albums continued. She has been a professional singer and celebrity for over fifty years, a remarkable span for one who shook too much to dance, and volunteered: "I'll sing!" The awards from fellow performers and many others have been countless. In 1982, Harvard's Hasty Pudding Club chose Ella as their Woman of the Year, gave her a standing ovation, and a chorus of "A Tisket, A Tasket," one of her trademark old songs. And, in 1990, she's still going.

Other Black singers who put their stamp on the 1940s and later were Billy Eckstine, Sarah Vaughan, Lena Horne, Dinah Washington and Pearl Bailey.

Pearl was born in 1918 in Newport News, Virginia. She made her stage debut in 1933, winning first prize in an amateur contest with a song and dance routine, which included "Poor Butterfly." At the Apollo Theater in Harlem, she won first prize again, with "Solitude." From there, she went on to appear as a special dance with Noble Sissle's orchestra, as a chorus girl in Washington and Baltimore nightclubs, and as a vocalist with such bands as Cootie Williams.

In 1944, at the Village Vanguard, in downtown New York City, she perfected the slow, leisurely style that became her trademark. A song called "Tired" expressed it in music. She made a stage debut in "St. Louis Woman," which earned her the Donaldson Award. To cap her career, she went to college.

Sarah Vaughan was born in Newark, New Jersey in 1924, and began music studies at age seven. In 1942, at age eighteen, she, like so many others, entered an amateur contest at the Apollo Theater. She sang "Body and Soul" and won first prize. Billy Eckstine convinced Earl "Fatha" Hines to hire her as a singer. In the late 1950s, she had her greatest hit, "Broken Hearted Melody." Not long ago, she was praised on the floor of the U.S. House of Representatives. She died of cancer on April 3, 1990.

Dinah Washington was still another amateur hour winner. From 1943 to 1946 she was featured vocalist with Lionel Hampton. She became one of the top female vocalists of the 1950s. Dinah Washington had a tremendous influence on the younger generation, especially upon Aretha Franklin. She was a fiery woman, who once beat up her husband, on stage, with his own saxophone. She sang and recorded jazz, blues, pop, and even country. Like too many others, a tempestuous life ended with an overdose in 1953, at the peak of her career.

Ray Charles has been a star for fifty years, a long time in a business where fame can be fleeting. More than anyone else, he helped to develop the rhythm and blues of the 1950s into the "soul" of the 1960s. Born in 1930, he was permanently blinded at age six. But he absorbed gospel and blues from church and bars; and jazz, swing, and country from the radio. His loss of sight perhaps contributed to a more acute sense of hearing, which he conveyed in his playing.

When his mother died, he was fifteen and quit school to become a full-time musician. Charles was greatly influenced by the work of Nat King Cole. His success climbed through the 1950s and peaked in 1959. His biggest hit was "Georgia On My Mind." After 1960, he was called "a living legend whose most seminal work is in the past."

Nat King Cole was another talent contestant and he may have been the youngest. He played piano in a contest in Montgomery, Alabama at age four. At five, he was playing church organ and piano for his minister-father. With his high school band, he made his singing debut when a customer insisted he sing "Sweet Lorraine," which he later made into a big hit. In the 1940s, he built a reputation with a jazz trio; but he became so much the standout that in 1948, when he recorded the solo hit "Nature Boy," the trio disbanded.

The suave ballad style became his trademark; so much so that a Nat King Cole recording seemed to evoke nostalgia, no matter what the theme. He had mass popular appeal with one velvet hit after another, and Christmas has not been the same since "The Christmas Song." He underwent lung surgery in January 1966, and died a month later. He lives on with records and tapes and through his daughter Natalie, who is a soul star in her own right.

Chuck Berry was born on October 18, 1926, in St. Louis. He became one of a handful of musicians who helped to create the rock revolution. Like Miles Davis, he came from solid middle class origins, different from the poverty of so many Black musicians.

A local R&B performer gave him an old guitar, a key event in his musical life. Muddy Waters "discovered" Berry in an East St. Louis club and his music evolved over a fifteen years period from 1940 to 1954. When he was finished, there began the golden age of rock, which he pioneered with Little Richard and others. Along the way, he developed his patented "duck walk," in which he sloped across the stage with his guitar.

1958 was Berry's top year and he was as popular in England as in the USA. It is said that the pressures of stardom changed his personality, and in 1961, he was jailed for an offense that was unfortunate in its doubtful blame. He was released in 1963 and made a comeback, but was considered nostalgia. By the 1970s and 1980s, he was a star again and his European audience remained always strong.

James Brown has recently returned to entertainment, after a regrettable absence. He is one of the most successful Black artists of all time and has been perhaps the most influential figure in modern Black music.

He was born in Georgia in 1933 and came to music by way of gospel. He soon began to record a chain of consecutive hits, and developed a stage act to match his music. He has been the pattern for all who followed. Unlike many others, he developed into an astute businessman, whose investments include several Black radio stations. At the same time, he has enjoyed enormous success in Britain.

He started off as an R&B singer in the 1950s, only to become the Father of Soul. He is at a turning point in his life, and the public will watch, with interest and good wishes, the nature of his return.

Chubby Checker exemplifies the performer who becomes typed with one single feature, the Twist, in 1960. When the public tired of it, Checker faded. Before he did, he was part of a humorous incident. A prominent U.S. Senator arrived at a midwest airport and saw a throng of young people surging toward him. Elated, he prepared to greet them. They surged right past him, to where Chubby Checker was following along. He was king for a day.

When Fats Domino was very young, a cousin left a piano at his house. Fats took it from there. His teens were spent playing and singing in local clubs and bars. He recorded a hit in 1949; and in 1955, he was "up on the charts." For the next eight years, he was prominent among the top recorders. Like so many others, he was a hit in Britain.

The Queen of Soul, Aretha Franklin, also had a preacher-father who promoted her to choir solo. She became a local celebrity. He took her on the road and into recording. She turned to secular music but the gospel influence came along. By 1967, she was "soul" as well as the outstanding Black female star. Ray Charles was her mentor and he can sometimes be heard in her music. Her success tracked exactly the great break-through in Black music, generally, in the 1960s. She has reverted a little to spirituals and R&B, but she is still Queen. She has toured Europe successfully.

Who invented rock? There are early indicators, but no one emerges as the single originator. Chuck Berry must be given a share of the credit. The term "rock and roll" had been used as early as 1951. From there, it is asserted that the first rock record was "Sh-Boom," recorded in 1954 by the Chords, and an instant hit. It seemed to be a blend of R&B, pop, country western, and something new.

There seems little doubt that rock was a Black creation to which whites gravitated and then acknowledged their debt. The Beatles were especially open in their gratitude. The origins of rock may be best understood by attention to the career of Little Richard.

Little Richard came on the American scene in 1955; it is said; "He single-handedly laid the formulations of a new music form, 'rock and roll.' He paved the way for performers like Michael Jackson, after being raised on gospel and spirituals.

His early records did not succeed. When his father died, he took a job washing dishes in the Greyhound bus station. But he eventually got a band together and found plenty of work. A song called "Tutti Frutti" took the public by storm. Leaving one band, he was replaced by a singer named James Brown.

By now, he was recording gold records and he starred in an early rock and roll movie, "Don't Knock the Rock."

After successfully touring Europe he retired briefly and returned to stardom in the early 1960s.

By this time, however, he was heavily into drugs and he quit the entertainment world and entered the ministry, from which he condemned rock and roll as an instrument of the devil. However, he is now very much back as a member of the entertainment world. His long term future will unfold. Did he invent rock and roll? Perhaps — together with a generation of young people.

For almost twenty years, from 1959 to 1967, the Supremes topped the charts all over the world. In 1964, their "Where Did Our Love Go?" bumped the Beatles out of first place. When Diana Ross became preeminent, she left the group in 1969, and embarked on a solo career. After a farewell concert in London, in 1976, the group disbanded. Of that occasion, one of the members, Mary Wilson, wrote: "It's amazing how many performers will stay in the states and suffer at the hands of a fickle record industry, while all over the world there are hundreds of thousands of fans dying to see them and buy their records."

Diana Ross had phenomenal success after leaving the Supremes. As a teenager, she (like many others) had tried out for a talent competition. Unlike others we have seen, she failed. She immediately formed her own group and started down the road to success. The group eventually became the Supremes, and from the Supremes, Diana Ross launched her solo career. Had she won the talent competition, would it all have happened? In 1972, she played Billie Holiday in "Lady Sings the Blues." She has drawn raves from critics, college students, and nightclub goers.

Matching the Supremes on the male side were the Temptations and their "Motown sound." An R&B group, they were organized in 1960, as a singing and dancing male quintet. In 1965, they had perhaps their biggest hit in "My Girl." They have traveled the United States and Europe, and have been regulars on radio and television. They still play to millions the world over.

Roberta Flack was born in 1940, and like so many others, she had her first musical inspiration in church. Her mother was a church organist. By age nine, she had acquired a taste for jazz, blues, and R&B. She also had a strong early interest in classical music. At age fifteen, she was awarded a full musical scholarship at Howard University. Her father's death interrupted her musical development and forced her into a series of teaching jobs. But when her musical career resumed, she demonstrated remarkable stamina and prolific output. One of her early auditions featured the recording of thirty-nine songs in nine hours. She made her first album in 1969.

In the early 1970s, Roberta Flack rose from a musical cult figure in Washington, DC, to one of the most popular female singers in the world. Her reputation flourished with one hit after another. Washington gave her "Roberta Flack Day" and the keys to the city.

Muddy Waters had two important possessions: his own talent and a desire to help other Black musicians. In every field of popular music, from rock to soul, he exerted tremendous influence. His encouragement of his band members led each one to become a star in his own right. So successful was he that the band members outsold Muddy Waters himself. He has probably been the most recorded of all blues artists.

Leslie Uggams is a fine pop singer, whose career began at age two on the old "Beulah" television show. She made her singing debut at age six in a New York church. At age nine, she sang in Harlem's Apollo Theater, and in 1961-64, she gained popularity on the "Sing Along with Mitch" television show. She is now nationally recognized and is active on radio, television, theater, nightclubs, and college campuses.

Ike and Tina Turner gradually came to mean Tina Turner, after they were organized in 1956. In 1959, she won acclaim for the song "Fool in Love." She has enjoyed wide popularity since then, and has toured the USA and Europe with the Rolling Stones. A "comeback" in 1985, at age 45, netted Tina three Grammies, a hit single, and a triple platinum album.

In 1980, Johnny Mathis celebrated twenty-five years of recording for Columbia Records. In the beginning, he was labeled a Black Frank Sinatra, far from the mainstream of Black music. Then suddenly, in the late 1970s, he became an authentic soul singer, a style which carried him through the 1980s. He was launched in 1958 when he recorded "A Certain Smile." His "Greatest Hits" album stayed on the best-seller charts for a record-breaking four hundred and ninety weeks.

B. B. King, also known as "The Blues King," knew how to solve a problem. He was unable to sing and play at the s%' (* so he developed a style in which he alternated powerful vocal lines with dazzling guitar licks. The style is now an integral part of blues tradition. Beginning in 1949, his records appeared almost every week.

In September 1990 he and other musical stars were honored in a White House ceremony with awards conferred by President Bush.

La Vern Baker was a fifties singer who recorded a whole string of hits, including pop, gospel, and blues. Although her records pointed the way to the soul era, she went into decline when soul became popular in the early 1960s. Now she is back in the news, prompted by her appearance at Washington's Kennedy Center on February 23, 1990. Now sixty, she has returned from a long absence in the Philippines to test the waters at home. She has received awards from the Rhythm and Blues Foundation. Her attitude toward music today is not always flattering. "The music today isn't lasting," she has said "If you can bark, you can make a living today. I've heard some singers — big singers making big bucks — that if they can sing, I can make a watch." At age sixty, with a style popular thirty-five years ago, La Vern Baker may need a very clever talent to register a comeback.

Harry Belafonte was born in New York City on March 1, 1927. He spent years eight to thirteen in the West Indies. He became a successful singer, but was dissatisfied with the music he was performing. He returned to New York City to study folk music. In the 1950s, he appeared often as a folk singer and was well-received. He pioneered integrated television musicals, won two Emmys, and was fired by the sponsor for his efforts. But in the 1960s and 1970s, he was on television again, and in the early 1980s he was touring the USA, Europe, and Australia.

Both parents of Gladys Knight sang with "Wings Over Jordan," and influenced her from her birth in 1944. She debuted as a gospel singer at age four, and won first place on television's Ted Mack Amateur Hour at age eight. From 1950 to 1953, she toured with the Morris Brown University Choir. In 1953, she became an original member of The Pips, a group later renamed Gladys Knight and the Pips.

Blind from birth, Stevie Wonder showed an early interest in music. By the age of eight, he was skilled on the drums, bongoes, piano, and harmonica. He signed his first recording contact at age nine, but he began to make his reputation through live appearances. As early as age thirteen, he was at the top of the charts. He has had the success in Britain which has been so characteristic of touring Black performers. He continues to perform live, on records, and on radio and television. His easy good nature attracts as many fans as does his musical talent — a talent that is matched by his talent in business.

A musician since age eight, Stevie Wonder was asked how he coped with the pressures of being a world leader in music. He replied: "That doesn't bother me. I knew what the job entailed before I took it."

Bob Marley was not born in the USA. He was born in Jamaica in 1945. In addition to popularizing reggae, he was a social activist and a minister to the oppressed. In the beginning, his school chums became his musical colleagues. He was also influenced by his mother, a gospel singer in a local church. In the USA, he made his first recording at age sixteen, but during the Vietnam War, he returned to Jamaica. He was extremely popular in Britain, where he often stood higher than in the USA.

His social and political involvements gave him an international stature which equaled his reputation in reggae. But he also became a target for factional gunmen. He was wounded in a 1976 assassination attempt, but went on to perform that evening. In 1981, he met a slow death from cancer, at age thirty-five.

The reggae which Marley made popular, with tours by Bob Marley and the Wailers, had many origins. It stemmed from Jamaican popular music, Afro-Jamaican music, Afro-American music, and North American pop and rock elements.

James Cliff, born in 1948, was another reggae singer. He appeared with a Jamaican group at the New York World's Fair in 1964. He was the lead actor in the first all-Jamaican movie. His style of reggae blended rock, calypso, soul, jazz, blues, and traditional African and religious music.

Earth, Wind, and Fire was a group of nine male vocalists who flourished in the 1970s, after being organized in 1969 by Maurice White. He had toured as a child with gospel singers and was exposed to jazz, blues, and rock in high school bands. Earth, Wind, and Fire demonstrated this variety of styles.

Al Green, born in 1946, was one of the most popular entertainers of the 1970s. He started out in a gospel quartet at age nine. He organized an R&B group in high school, and they toured the South and the Midwest. He began to record in 1967, and his recordings carried him to the top. Like many others, he toured extensively in the USA and in Europe, employing a style much influenced by James Brown. He has been regarded as highly individualistic, even eccentric.

Jimi Hendrix died in 1970 at age twenty-seven. Before he died, he made a sensational mark as a Black musician. When he was thirteen, he was given a guitar and taught himself to play by listening to recordings. It was in the U.S. Air Force that he developed a distinctive performance style. Later, he toured with Tina Turner, the Isley Brothers, and James Brown's back-up group. His hallmark was that of flashy attire, electronic gadgetry, ear-shattering volume, and antics. He toured Europe in 1966, and when he came home in the following year, he had an immense following. He was featured at the Woodstock Festival and was easily regarded as the most gifted rock performer of the 1960s.

Miriam Zenzi Makeba was born in South Africa, in 1932. Her early folksinging performances were there. She made her television debut on the BBC in 1959 and became a protege of Harry Belafonte, who brought her to the USA, to tour. Her American television debut occurred on the Steve Allen Show in 1959. She became an international entertainer, singing a wide range of material, from jazz to the songs of her native Xhosa nation.

Billy Preston, born in 1946, is a keyboard musician as well as a singer. He learned piano at three and organ at six. He gained early experience by singing in gospel choirs. At age ten, he appeared in concert with Mahalia Jackson. In "St. Louis Blues," he played W. C. Handy as a boy. In the early 1960s, he toured the USA as an R&B performer. He also performed with Ray Charles, The Beatles and The Rolling Stones. By the 1970s, he was a leading rock entertainer.

Charley Pride, born in 1939, was the first Black to have a successful career in country and western music. He listened to the Grand Old Opry as a child, and learned to sing along with the country singers. When his fame as a singer spread, he himself debuted with the Grand Old Opry.

Otis Redding, born in 1941, was killed in a plane crash at the peak of his career. From a church choir, he went professional in the early 1960s, and by 1965, was a leading R&B singer.

The Isley Brothers began as gospel vocalists, performing with their pianist mother. With her blessing, they left Cincinnati for New York City, and a career in secular music. By 1957, they had top engagements in Washington, DC and New York City. Their recording career was slow to take off, but it finally did and in 1969 they went to the top of the charts with a non-stop series of hits. In the period 1973 to 1981, they sold twelve million albums, without any drastic change in style, and without touring outside the USA.

Sam Cooke has also been called the Father of Soul. His hits were fewer than those of Fats Domino or James Brown, but he had a far greater influence on other artists. Gospel was his early specialty, in the period 1950-1956. Later he blended gospel, soul, R&B, blues, and pop. He was slain in December, 1964.

Since the 1950s, The Drifters have been one of the best-loved Black vocal groups ever to emerge. Their hits are in the dozens, and their popularity in Britain has at times exceeded their popularity in the USA.

In 1967, Nina Simone, was "Female Jazz Singer of the Year." Born in 1935, she is an original and versatile Black concert performer. She first showed virtuosity on the piano. Later came success as a vocalist and a composer.

The pop quartets, active until very recently, evoke a special nostalgia not only because of their endurance as performers, but because of the warmth and grace with which they perform. The Mills Brothers were successful and active from 1922 to well into the 1980s. With a unique singing style, they became the first Black singing group to win commercial sponsorship on a nationwide network. They registered a series of hits including "Paper Doll", "Up the Lazy River," "Glow Worm" and "Goodbye Blues." The Ink Spots were organized in 1934, and were first recognized in England. Returning to the USA in 1939, they recorded the hit "If I Didn't Care," in their usual smooth harmonies. They were active into the 1980s.

Michael Jackson came out of The Jackson Five. It has been observed that Black American music has often been fostered by the family structure, especially family gospel groups. So it was with the Jacksons, who followed The Staple Singers, The Franklin Girls, The Emotions, The Isley Brothers, and Gladys Knight and the Pips.

Michael Jackson's success has been so unparalleled that one album, "Thriller," has sold over 40 million copies. One million copies, referred to as a "gold," record, were sold in Los Angeles alone. He received commendations from both the United States House and Senate for his contributions to American youth.

His personal life suffered because of his fame, which is not unusual for an entertainer. It was said that his only friends were his brothers. But his artistic gifts continue to be showered on an appreciative audience, which has been loyal for over two decades. He has shared the heights with only a few others. He is phenomenally popular in Japan.

Chapter Thirteen

Banding Together

Chapter Thirteen

Banding Together

Accustomed to initiating and introducing such captivating music forms as jazz and blues, Black musicians found it more difficult to enter upon the world of the big bands, which was already established. When they did succeed, they brought a new drive, a spirit, and a feeling among themselves and their listeners that it was all an adventure.

In the beginning, the odds were long. The difficulties of travel and accommodations were an example. One musician reported that Black bands would seek out the houses of prostitution as the cleanest places to which they would be admitted. In time, their talent and their music helped to wear down much of the racial intolerance which made the beginning so much of an effort.

Fletcher Henderson, born at the end of the nineteenth century, is credited with being the first important Black leader of a big band. His orchestra has been called the most delightful and irresponsible ever assembled. Henderson's first job was as piano player, plugging songs at the W. C. Handy Music Company; and then and there, he cast his future with music.

In 1923, Handy sent him on the road as accompanist to Ethel Waters. The tour ended badly, and Henderson was stranded and broke, somewhere in the Midwest. Eventually, in the same year, he won a contract with an established club and assembled a real band. But he was neither a businessman nor a disciplinarian, and his fortunes and his attention to music fluctuated from year to year. Drunken musicians periodically fell off the bandstand, but there was enough on the solid side to make the orchestra great. His reputation as an arranger brought Henderson added fame.

He spent a few months with Benny Goodman in 1939, and by 1948, he had come full circle and was back on the road with Ethel Waters. In 1950, he suffered the stroke which kept him bed-ridden until his death in 1952.

Charley Cook earned a doctorate from the American Conservatory. When he started his band in 1920, he called his group: "Charley Cook and his Fourteen Doctors of Syncopation"." His orchestra became the best known of the "Chicago Bands." They broadcast regularly on radio, but by 1930, the Great Depression had done him in. Ironically, at his final performance, all the band's instruments were stolen.

Jimmy Europe migrated to New York City in 1904, where he found plenty of work as an orchestra director. He first had his own eleven-piece society orchestra, and then formed an association with the Castle dance team. World War I found him in uniform, and he organized a large regimental band, recognized as the finest marching group of the war years. Back in the United States at age forty, he was fatally stabbed by one of his own dance band members, on May 19, 1919.

Duke Ellington has been well described in an earlier chapter. Suffice it to say that his music was consistently classic. Count Basie has also been well described. The coming on the scene of so many rare talents within the same time frame is striking.

Noble Sissle was born in 1889 and had his first good luck right in his hometown of Indianapolis. The manager of a hotel had seen quality hotel bands in the East, and commissioned one for his hotel. After meeting the test, Sissle went East himself, to Baltimore, where he made his first recordings in 1916. Then he went to Paris, where he remained until 1920. In 1921, he organized "Noble Sissle and His Sizzling Syncopators," and the group remained intact until 1925.

Sissle then went to London for five years and when he returned his band had a distinctly international flavor. His was thought of as a "society orchestra," and a top one that recorded copiously. He was active when he died in his eighties.

To this point, Louis Armstrong has been presented largely as a solo performer. But he spent years in the big band arena. He joined his first big band, Fletcher Henderson's, in 1924. At that time, it was a pioneering band and a good one, to which Louis contributed substantially. After a year, however, he returned to Chicago and did not return to the big band format until 1930, when he began recording activity in Los Angeles. He remained in the big band arena until 1947. He often fronted for groups directed by others, and just as often he was thought to be the leader.

Chick Webb and His Chicks was an orchestra that grew as orchestras grew generally, without any effort to be out front. By 1934, his group was playing at The Savoy, and he was taking Ella Fitzgerald out of an orphanage and giving her a job. She, in turn, helped him to fame. He became known as the "King of Drums."

In 1937, at The Savoy, there occurred the Great Competition between the orchestras of Chick Webb and Benny Goodman. A near-riot resulted as each orchestra tried to generate more and more applause, as each group alternated on the bandstand. Despite the participation of Ziggy Elmna, Goodman, and Gene Kruppa, Webb's orchestra won easily, leaving Goodman in disbelief.

Chick Webb died in June of 1939 and Ella Fitzgerald took over the orchestra. She changed it from a fraternity to a business enterprise, and drove them hard. In 1942, the orchestra disbanded, with members no longer willing to sacrifice or endure.

Fats Waller's talented life included eight years of big band activity. Because his orchestra did little recording, those years, from 1935 to 1943, were not memorable.

Erskine Hawkins assembled a big band from high school musicians and they opened at the Harlem Opera House in 1935. In the beginning they were sponsored by the Alabama State Teachers College, but they were on their own by 1936. By 1937, they were highly successful and working fifty weeks out of the year. They became an established attraction at The Savoy and scored many hit recordings. An impromptu recording, "Tuxedo Junction," became an exceptional hit. They entered into "battles" with both Lionel Hampton and Duke Ellington. Hawkins' young band lost to them both, but by very little. When The Savoy closed in the late 1950s, the Erskine Hawkins orchestra disbanded.

Lionel Hampton's big band activity has already been described. An additional note should include that his use of noise, lights, and other exciting features were forerunners of rock and roll.

Cab Calloway could neither read music nor play an instrument, but he led a big band, and a good one; and he could sing.

In March, 1931, when he was twenty-four, he made a single recording which established him. He led a succession of early big bands, insisting on conservatism in jazz and resisting new music. His records were extremely popular during World War II and he was active for decades thereafter, with orchestras large and small.

Jimmie Lunceford's orchestra, for a few brief years in the 1930s, was one of the most exciting big bands that ever played. As a high school music instructor in New York City, he selected and assembled talent, gradually forming a big band around him.

The Lunceford band was both tightly rehearsed and loose enough to swing; and its arrangements were a constant surprise, both in originality and in treatment of pop songs. Precision was a hallmark, even when trumpeters threw their horns in the air and caught them in exact formation. Although Lunceford could play saxophone, clarinet, flute, trombone, guitar, and banjo, he never played with the band. His basic role was as the father of a musical family. For a time, the band broadcast several times a week from The Cotton Club.

Somehow, the large amounts of money coming in were not filtering down to the musicians and toward the end of the 1930s, disintegration set in. But Jimmie Lunceford kept a band together until his death of a heart attack, at age forty-five, in July 1947. His music is performed today by the American Jazz Orchestra.

Earl "Fatha" Hines was a brilliant pianist and led one of the foremost bands of the 1920s, 1930s, and 1940s. He played much more jazz than sweet music. Born in 1905, he was performing in Chicago by 1922. He and his bands were often controlled and manipulated by the Capone mob. At times, Charlie "Bird" Parker, Billy Eckstine, and Sarah Vaughan performed with the orchestra. In 1948, the band was dissolved.

This happened despite the fact that Hines stayed out front and was very receptive to the bop era.

Dizzy Gillespie we have seen. His big band troubles ended when he stopped playing where he didn't fit and teamed with musicians of the same spirit and dedication to the new music. He emerged as the High Priest of Bop.

Chapter Fourteen

Very Recently

Chapter Fourteen

Very Recently

A trip down memory lane can be a gift to the present. So it was on December 10, 1989, when Dizzy Gillespie and Billy Eckstine reunited after forty years of successful solo careers. On that day, they combined their talents with the Count Basie Orchestra for a concert of be-bop and blues, as a salute to the Count who had died the previous spring.

Dizzy Gillespie reminisced about his collaboration with Eckstine in the early 1940s, and about the genius of Count Basie: "The best tempo in the world. He got it right every time." Almost fifty years later, he was alive in the music of two colleagues, and in the hearts of a hall full of fortunate listeners.

In the same general time period, the *Washington Post* reported "R&B's Cure for the Blues." It described the creation of the Rhythm and Blues Foundation, which seeks to foster greater recognition and financial support for R&B musicians of the 1940s, 1950s, and 1960s. The Smithsonian Museum of American History extended an official salute to the Foundation, and an awards ceremony to honor past greatness was organized.

La Vern Baker, a former great in R&B who is seeking to come back, said simply of the foundation: "This way you can always keep your head up with dignity."

Nostalgia for R&B runs deep. A former music store owner in the Washington area gathered greats from long-time groups of the 1950s and 1960s and recorded a Christmas collector's album for 1989, featuring doo-wop and bop. One old performer said of the groups of the day: "They were our idols, they were the ones who made us feel like we were someone . . ." Another said: "There are certain musics, in my opinion, that are trendy . . . they disappear, but this 50s stuff and the R&B, it comes back year after year."

John Cephas, in September of 1989, won one of thirteen National Heritage Fellowships bestowed at that time by the National Endowment for the Arts. John Cephas, at age fifty-nine, is a bluesman, a guitarist. In honoring him, the Endowment is also honoring the blues tradition, which has had such an impact on other American music. With the same sense of indebtedness, the U.S. State Department has sponsored Cephas on tours of Africa, Europe, South and Central America, China, the Soviet Union, and Australia.

His mother gave him an early and intense exposure to religious music. After a life in the blues, he is sad that blues seems to be disappearing among the people from whom it sprang. But he presses on. A new album was released in the Fall of 1989; more world tours are planned; and he firmly believes there are new fans to be made.

In the Fall of 1989, an opera made its world debut at the Warner Theater in Washington, DC. It was "Long Tongues: A Saxophone Opera"; and the guiding genius was Julius Hemphill. Matching his personality, the opera was unorthodox in every respect. Arias were sung by six saxophones, with no human voices at all. The composer is fifty-one years old, and dislikes rules of any kind, particularly in music. But there is the impression that as he gets older, he is less interested in knocking tradition and more interested in entertaining. Multiply Julius Hemphill by the thousands and there is an inkling of the creative talent still active in the world of Black music.

An example is the veteran tenor saxophonist, Stanley Turrentine. At fifty-five, in January, 1990, he put together a major fundraising concert at the Apollo Theater in New York. It was for the benefit of the homeless and recovering alcoholics. His concert schedule takes him far and wide and he plans to teach at the Duke Ellington School of the Arts.

Turrentine remembers, as a very young man, stealing into after-hours clubs where top musicians came to jam. He heard Art Tatum, Nat King Cole, Charlie "Bird" Parker, Lester Young, Don Byas, Illinois Jacquet, and others. He recalls that they were glad to help him, and that Nat King Cole taught him the verses to "Stardust." He was also encouraged at home, where his father played tenor saxophone and clarinet. His mother and sisters played piano and violin. He himself started out on the cello, but he would put it in the corner and pick up the saxophone. He put together his first group in high school, "Four Bees and a Bop." His career since — thirty years of it — has been a satisfaction and a success. One secret to his success has been his habit of learning well the lyrics to the songs he plays. "Then I try to play lyrically."

The *Washington Post* of March 4, 1990, tells of two young Black musicians, as if from another era. They are the Harper Brothers, Philip and Winard. "They caress standards and blues in the dark, smoke-filled nightclubs of New York and Washington . . . Like the current generation of young jazz artists . . . they play bop the way it used to be played . . . reminiscent of early Miles Davis."

What they hear from listeners, after they play, is: "I don't like jazz but I like this." The Harpers respect music, and regret that quality has disappeared in recent years. Perhaps they are right, or perhaps there have been changes in the notion of what quality is.

Ebony Magazine is a rich source of information on Black musicians, as a perusal of issues from the past few years will bear out. No music form escapes its attention.

The May, 1988, edition, for example, comments on The Winans, who excel as three-time Grammy winners, and as trendsetters who meet resistance from traditionalists. And the Clark Sisters, who have developed an updated rocking gospel sound that won them a prestigious award in 1987. Another gospel legend is Shirley Greene, who mixes the contemporary with the traditional, and very successfully. She has twenty-five albums. "More and more, gospel takes on an R&B sound. Wise heads say that gospel must stay current to survive. Other wise heads take a 'no compromise' stance."

Other issues include items equally interesting. Patti LaBelle is described as an electrifying performer whose concerts are standing-room only. There is praise not only for her vocal talents, but for her wonderful rapport with her audiences.

Sallie Martin, ninety years old in 1986, and the mother of gospel music, has been praised from coast to coast. She blazed the trail when gospel had no popularity, in the 1930s and 1940s. Purists said that the influence of jazz made it the devil's music. For nearly sixty years, Sally traveled the USA and abroad, as a solo and in a group. She was a long-time collaborator with Thomas A. Dorsey, who discovered her in 1929 at a choir rehearsal in a Chicago home.

The Barrett Sisters, proponents of traditional gospel, have been called "house wreckers," both for packing in an audience and for the power they put into their singing. Yet, there is concern that the gospel message will be lost in contemporary sound.

Michael Jackson's humanitarian efforts are described as keeping pace with his musical progress. He has given $600,000 to the United Negro College Fund. He received an award from President Reagan for his work in the anti-drunk-driving campaign, and he received an honorary doctorate from Fisk University. In another place, *Ebony* reports on Michael Jackson's last tour, over $125 million earned. The question arises, "Will he retire?"

New York-born Terence Trent D'Arby mixes soul and pop. His first album was a double platinum. His father was an evangelical preacher and his mother was a gospel singer. With disarming honesty, he admits to an early desire for attention.

Diana Reeves who is thirty-four years old, has given jazz a sophisticated sound which has drawn large audiences. She is the first Black female jazz singer to ever perform in the Soviet Union. In addition to jazz, she sings electric pop, West Indian, West African, and Brazilian music.

John Coltrane is remembered as one of the jazz world's most innovative musicians. His early work with Dizzy Gillespie, Miles Davis, and Thelonius Monk is cited; he died from cancer, in 1967, at the age of forty-one.

Herbie Hancock's story reflects twenty-seven years of walking the tightrope between jazz and pop — a balancing act he has accomplished with a very skilled piano, further balanced between acoustic and electronic music. In his late forties, he has fifty albums and has recorded on one hundred and fifty others. His new and younger fans know him as the master of high-tech funk.

He won an 1984 Grammy Award for his single, "Rocket." Older fans like the acoustic master who played with Miles Davis in the 1960s. He has the fascinating dream of one day adding classical music to his repertoire. He says: "Just because I'm so interested in the future, it doesn't mean I'm giving up any skills I acquired in the past."

"Everybody likes the blues, whether they know it or not." That's a quote from *Ebony*, which also cites the blues skills of harmonica player Bill Branch, and Koko Taylor, the reigning "Queen of the Blues" in Chicago.

Kool and the Gang was one of the hottest groups of the 1980s, and they saw music as a vehicle for getting involved in many social causes. "Cherish" was a top hit of 1985.

Anita Baker, described in 1986 as "Soul's New Romantic Singer," had abandoned music in 1981, but a recording contract drew her back. She has been praised for the passion of her delivery, the clarity of her lyrics, and her modesty. She says: "People pay and they deserve a good concert."

In October, 1987, *Ebony* asked: "Who's the Greatest — Janet Jackson, Whitney Houston, or Anita Baker?"

In 1985, The Cotton Club, closed for forty-five years, was "revisited." Duke Ellington found it a springboard to success. Louis Armstrong and Cab Calloway created magic and gained national prominence. Ethel Waters introduced "Stormy Weather," and Lena Horne got her start there. Old members of the chorus line were interviewed. They remember Duke Ellington as a "delightful man who treated all the girls as ladies." Cab Calloway was remembered as "a wild one who was always joshing us." Louis Armstrong married a Cotton Club dancer.

Whitney Houston's first album was double platinum, as she rose to stardom in 1985. With that, and the sequel 2½ years later, she garnered 8 consecutive number 1 hits, surpassing records set by Elvis, the Beatles, and Diana Ross. Many credit her popularity as the factor which caused MTV to finally begin featuring the music and videos of black artists.

Her mother, Cissy, was a long-time pop and gospel singer, and Whitney was already traveling with her by the time she was 4. "The greatest sessions I remember were Aretha (Franklin's), she says. "They were so full of energy." Whitney learned to sing early, in the local Baptist church, first soloing there at age 11; and gospel music had the greatest influence on her life. At twelve, she set her sights on a singing career, touring with her mother, and made her Carnegie Hall debut at age 15. Her parents, however, would not permit a singing career to come before her education. Although she enjoyed a brief modelling career, her heart was set on music, to which she returned when she completed high school.

Dionne Warwick, her aunt, claims Whitney's success will never go to her head: "We won't let anybody stray that far . . . we always get back to reality." Now a multi-millionairess in her late twenties, she is praised for "exceptional talent, healthy good looks, and a clean-cut image."

Janet Jackson is another solo from the Jackson family. She started performing with her famous siblings at age nine, and is one of the few Black female artists to hit the top spot on *Billboard* magazine's pop album chart. She ranks in the top three of Black female singers.

In 1942, Billy Daniels volunteered to sing a song in the Club Harlem in Atlantic City, and "everybody just went crazy." In 1985, he was still performing forty weeks of the year. His treatment of Johnny Mercer's "Old Black Magic" is a masterpiece.

Prince is described as a trend setter, an avant-garde artist with broad appeal. He is the "something different" music fans always seek. Sheila E. is the hot drummer of pop rock, who opened for Prince in his phenomenally successful "Purple Rain" tour, in the Fall of 1984.

Quincy Jones, now in his late 50s, played the drums in Billie Holiday's band, at age fifteen. Since then he has had one success after another — as musician, composer, arranger, conductor, and record producer. He has written the music scores for fifty movies, including the critically acclaimed *The Color Purple*, and won an Emmy for the score of *Roots*. He is perhaps best known as the producer of Michael Jackson's *Thriller* album (at 40 million copies worldwide, the largest-selling album in history), and the person most responsible for the phenomenal *We Are the World*, which raised $50 million to combat world hunger.

Born in Chicago, his family moved to Seattle when he was 5. Growing up he became obsessed with his high school band. "I was curious about orchestration . . . How could that many people play together and not be playing the same notes?" But like his professional success later in life, he was not content to be merely an observer. ". . . I got totally obsessed with playing. I would stay in the band room all day and play everything. Piano. Percussion. Tuba. French horn. Alto horn, and finally trumpet." This last instrument is the one for which he is best known as a performer.

At 14, Jones met Ray Charles, then 16, who had just moved from Florida. The two of them lied about their ages in order to play in clubs, and Ray taught Quincy to write arrangements — in braille. Asked to join Lionel Hampton's band at 15, he didn't quite make it. Quincy remembers, "I was ready to go. I had my little trumpet bag, and I sat for three hours on the band bus." — when Mrs. Hampton threw him off, instructing him to stay in school.

Taking her advice, Quincy finished high school and entered Seattle University, transferring after just one semester to the Berklee College of Music, in Boston, on a full scholarship. After playing jazz clubs and building a solid reputation, he finally joined Hampton's band.

Twenty years later, after surviving surgery to correct a brain aneurysm, Quincy re-evaluated his life. Although he had worked with legends such as Tommy Dorsey, Dizzy Gillespie, Sammy Davis Jr., Count Basie, and Duke Ellington, worked as the first black executive at an established record company (Mercury), produced pop-rock performers, his own jazz-fusion compositions, and scored movies, he was not satisfied. He felt he still had important work to complete, and perhaps little time in which to do it. Advised by doctors not to perform, or risk another aneurysm, during the next 12 years he produced, among others, Michael Jackson's *Off the Wall*, *Thriller*, and *Bad* albums, as well as *We Are the World*.

But by 1986 his third marriage, to actress Peggy Lipton (Mod Squad, Twin Peaks) was failing, and he was exhausted from work and emotional pressure. Starting with a retreat to Tahiti at the invitation of friend Marlon Brando, over the next two years he restored his confidence and revitalized his spirit. He now says his life is in his own hands. At present, he is releasing his first performance album in eight years and producing two new television shows.

Barbra Streisand says he displays "as much integrity personally as he does professionally." Ray Charles says "He doesn't have one strand of evil hair in his head." And writer Wallace Terry wrote in *Parade*, "In a world of egos larger than life, I found a man as modest as a monk, obviously more comfortable making music than talking about himself." Duke Ellington described his music as "beyond category," and Michael Jackson called him simply, "a genius."

Perhaps his own words to Wallace Terry, however, are most enlightening:

> I feel like the most blessed person in the world. I worked with the first team of American music — Louis, Duke, Basie, Ella, Sarah, Milles, Dizzy, Eckstine, Sinatra — right up to all the kids around now, like Kool Moe Dee and Michael Jackson.
>
> I know there are some real bad racial things happening out there that are polarizing some of us. And that freaks me out. But consider what happened to Michael Jackson in the '80s. Little kids all over the globe had a black hero. That changed the truth about the world in which we live.
>
> You know, we have a culture that is vastly underrated. Especially by us Americans, black and white. We don't have a clue as to what it's about. The Europeans know. The world knows.
>
> There is a statue of [jazz saxophonist] Sidney Bechet in Paris. When the Europeans come over here, they expect to see statues of Charlie Parker or Louis Armstrong in front of Radio City. But we just think of them as a couple of black dudes who played nice. And black people, we have no sense of our musical history. And that's a shame, man. I just hope, before I get out of this world, I can do something about it. One thing we can look up to with pride is our heritage. That is a legacy that the whole world admires.

By his own standards, Jones' accomplishments are prodigious, and he has set a standard that others will admire and emulate. The respect given to performers such as Michael Jackson is in no small way due to his own efforts.

Tracy Chapman fills the pages of *Time* magazine for March 12, 1990. "Armed only with her voice, her guitar, and her conscience, Tracy Chapman has helped make protest music fashionable again." She is a twenty-four-year-old Tufts University graduate, who has won three Grammy Awards, including "Best New Artist." She has crisscrossed the globe with Sting, Bruce

Springsteen, and Peter Gabriel. She has quickly become a "cultural icon."

Her first ambition was to play the drums but her mother feared the noise and bought her a tinny $20 guitar. The instrument harmonized with her soul. Today, she is less than thrilled about fame. She tries to protect what she keeps inside. Although she has written hundreds of songs, she says that "there are a lot of things that you never show anyone else."

Frank Morgan is "an ex-con and a great sax." His early teacher was Charlie "Bird" Parker, and at seventeen he became addicted to the heroin that killed Parker. A cycle of prison, release, and relapse went on for thirty years. But in the mid-1980s, he began to get the upper hand on drugs and his pure playing now reflects the enthusiasm of a rookie. At fifty-six (in 1990), he seems anxious to recover lost time. He is praised by critics and other jazzmen.

He was seven years old when his father, a guitarist with the Ink Spots, took him to see Charlie Parker. His very young life was changed then and there. "His horn got a choke-hold on my heart," he says. Parker told him that if small hands want to learn the alto sax, they had best start off with the clarinet. Morgan got one the next day, and in three days he was ready for the alto sax!

At fifteen, he was offered the alto sax chair with Parker, but his father thought him too young. Soon, however, he was at the Club Alabam, backing Billie Holiday and Josephine Baker. He went to heroin to "bring out the Bird in me," but when Parker found out, he wept. Now he says: "All I have to do is stay healthy and play my horn, and everything else will flow from there."

In earlier pages, we read "Bunk" Johnson's description of the origins of jazz in 1895 and 1896. Almost a century later, two items appeared in *Time* magazine (February 12, 1990) which build a musical bridge across the years. One item describes the new release of classic "Bunk" Johnson sides, recorded during his remarkable comeback in the 1940s. They are said to capture "the remarkable tone and timing of the man who was Louis Armstrong's early idol." In the same issue of Time, there is a small article on a nineteen-year old Black female singer of the 1990s. Her name is Michel'le and she could be Bunk Johnson's great-grand daughter. They cheer when she sings. At twelve she began putting on shows in her parents' Los Angeles garage. "No More Lies" became a hot song and Michel'le is on the brink of real success. "If I get big, that's fine, but it's not my goal."

In the world of music today, it is a little pointless to say the word, Marsalis. At least without defining the word: Which Marsalis?

Do you main *Wynton Marsalis*, owner of honors like Jazz Musician of the Year, Jazz Album of the Year, No. 1 Trumpet, and typically described by a music critic as a trumpeter who will surely become one of this century's most distinguished careers in music. Eight-time Grammy Award winner, Wynton is probably the most successful and visible jazz musician of the last 20 years.

But, of course, when you say Marsalis, you may mean *Branford Marsalis*. Eldest of six brothers, four of whom are jazz musicians, he attended Berklee School of Music in Boston, played sax in Art Blakey's band, the Lionel Hampton Orchestra, Clark Terry's band, and brother Wynton's band — which he finally left to play with rock star, Sting. Although he has appeared in three movies, it was his music talent that caught the ear of Dr. George Butler, a CBS Records vice president and executive producer of jazz and progressive music, and earned a CBS contract.

Marsalis also means noted jazz pianist and composer, *Ellis*, the gifted and dedicated father, in this "First Family of Jazz;" nor should we forget brother *Delfeayo* (trombone player and producer) and youngest brother, *Jason*. Asked which of his sons was the best musician, Ellis Marsalis once was said to have replied "Well, Branford is the most talented, but Wynton *works harder*."

If only one person could claim the title "consummate entertainer," that person would be *Sammy Davis, Jr.* Dancer, actor, hipster, cultural phenomenon — yes, all of these. But all of these and much, much more. A singer who thrilled and inspired millions, from saloons to majestic symphonic halls. The entertainer's entertainer, he will be with us as long as there is music.

With that velvety baritone, *Lou Rawls* has not just entertained but mesmerized listeners for nearly 30 years, with 58 albums and three R&B Grammys. There are probably few, if any, lovers of popular American music who would not immediately recognize his rendition of "When the Lights Go Down Low." Even Chicago has named a street after this world famous singer and humanitarian, who has raised more than $60 million for the United Negro College Fund, through his annual "Lou Rawls Parade of Stars."

Milton John Hinton started his music career on the violin, at the age of 13; a few years later he turned to the bass horn; and then again to a curly maple-backed bass, with which he's been thrilling the music world at the heart of big bands led by Cab Calloway, Count Basie, and Duke Ellington, and with soloists ranging from Billie Holliday to Branford Marsalis. He's made more than 600 recordings, while, at the same time, playing a major role in the integration of television, radio, and studio session orchestras. And at Manhattan's Hunter and Baruch colleges he's busy instilling classic jazz values in every kind of instrumentalist.

The *Modern Jazz Quartet* (or MJQ) is an American music classic among any list of "classics" that anyone might put together. With *John Lewis* at the piano; *Milt Jackson* at the vibraphone; *Connie Kay*, the drums; and *Percy Heath*, the bass, the M.J.Q contributes an enduring capital "C" to the word "classic" and capital "M" to the word "music."

Famed Motown singer and legendary crooner *Smokey Robinson* has also experienced legendary ups and downs: On top of the world with the Miracles and in addition to penning most of that group's songs, Smokey wrote hits for The Temptations; and then went solo and enjoyed tremendous success in this medium, too. One of four music giants honored at the star-studded Grammy Living Legends Salute in Hollywood, he was described as a poet, songwriter, and legendary artist; one who combined rhythm and blues and pop music into a special sound that has been listened to for almost four decades.

Finally, in August of 1990, the Lincoln Center did what it undoubtedly should have done long ago: It commissioned its first jazz composition for a Classical Jazz concert and its composer and conductor was a living legend by the name of *Benny Carter*. Though the Lincoln Center recognition was late, other great musicians acknowledged Benny Carter's great talent many years ago: including Fletcher Henderson, Duke Ellington, and Benny Goodman, for whom he wrote countless arrangements. But amidst all of this tribute, one should not forget Benny Carter's own alto saxophone style, with its nuances of tone and attack.

At the same time, indeed, at the same Benny Carter concert, *Bobby Hutcherson* worked his very special magic on the vibes, showcasing Carter's affinity for complex harmonies and varied rhythms.

Fred Wesley, who thought of himself as a funk trombonist of the '70s, now wants to be known as the jazz trombonist of the

Very Recently

'90s. Starting almost one-third of a century ago, Wesley played in his father's big band; then one-nighters with The Ike and Tina Turner Revue. Following that, a tour in the Army found him in Alabama's 55th Army Band; and now as James Brown's Sideman and arranger. You can be sure there will be more of Fred Wesley's trombone — much more.

So much has changed since 1895. Everything but the essence — the desire to share feelings with music. And Black musicians have done it in a way so special, so distinctive, that the world has listened.

Chapter Fifteen

Rap or "Hip Hop"

Chapter Fifteen

Rap or "Hip Hop"

Lionel Hampton recently referred to "this rap trash." Trash it may be to many; but at this writing, it is "the rage" to many others. Can it be that some have come full circle to the primitive African drum, to a world where melody, perhaps even music, does not exist? The beat predominates and, it is said, makes for excellent dancing. If each generation needs its own music, then what do the newest forms say? These questions are easy to ask, but are hard to answer. It may be sufficient now to simply describe rap and house music. Some answers may emerge.

Public Enemy; Tone-Loc; Run DMC; L.L. Cool J; 2 Live Crew; Salt 'n' Peppa; D. J. Jazzy Jeff and the Fresh Prince; De La Soul; NWA; SIW; Kool Moe Dee — these are some of the rap groups prominent in 1990.

Rap, or hip-hop to its fans, has grown into the most exciting development in American pop music in more than a decade. The biggest pop single of 1989 was a rap song by Tone-Loc, "Wild Thing," which sold two million copies.

The basic sound, propelled by a slamming polyrhythmic beat, is loud and raw. The lyrics, spoken, are a raucous stew of street-corner bravado, boisterousness, profanity, sex, vulgarity, bigotry, and insult. At times it is socially constructive. Adherents say that the dancing which accompanies the "song" is an important part of enjoyment.

The Grammy Awards have created a new rap music category. There is the recognition that whatever individual views there may be, rap is the first important cultural development in twenty-five years that the baby-boom generation didn't pioneer.

Students of rap say that with the passage of time it sounds less and less like "normal" music, possibly to keep outsiders outside. It is also considered by many to be a positive social outlet among many that are worse. Political consciousness is an ever-stronger expression, and the failure to stress it can cost a group its popularity. At the age of twenty-two, L.L. Cool J is passe, because he "wanted to take people's minds away from it."

"Even at its scariest, rap may be a safety valve rather than an opened floodgate." In any event, expectations that it will change soon are akin to "telling blues singers to lighten up."

House music has been described as "Boom! Boom! Boom! Boom!" More precisely, it is a mechanized bass drum, pounding incessantly at one hundred and twenty beats per minute, amplified to earth-shaking volume. The beat is accompanied by words, but seldom by a story, as in rap. It is also said to be easy to dance to.

House music was created in the Black discos of Chicago in the mid-1980s. For a long time, it stayed underground. In early 1990, however, a group called Techtronics scored a runaway hit called "Pump Up the Jam." As a result, many are predicting that radio's Top 40 will open up to house music in the way it eventually opened up to rap. If so, house music may move out of the clubs. If so, the audiences, captive or otherwise, should be prepared for a sound that "blows out the speakers."

Finally, there is a hot new style called "hip-house" which combines both rap and house. The bass is king, but there is some evidence that some groups, seemingly so new, are branching out at R&B and other forms already. The group Ten City is beginning to concentrate on meaningful lyrics and sophisticated melodies. For those who retain a liking for "normal" music, that is music to their ears.

A Postlude

In April, 1945, a photograph was widely published in newspapers and magazines across the country. The scene was Warm Springs, Georgia, as the body of Franklin D. Roosevelt was carried to the train on the day after his death. Pictured was Chief Petty Officer Graham Jackson, a black staff member, who saluted F.D.R.'s passage on his accordion.

Jackson's head was high in grief and loss, as tears streamed down his face. With the grief, however, was pride — in himself and in his art. In so many ways, he was the picture of the black musician, with origins in the slave quarters, and then struggling toward freedom. In the fall of 1989, *Time* magazine published "150 Years of Photo Journalism," and Jackson's grieving photograph was included. It remains a symbol of one hundred and fifty years of the Black musician, but with happier moments since.

Bibliography
and
Index

Bibliography

Reflections on Afro-American Music. Dominique-Rene de
    Lerma, Kent State University Press, 1973

The Negro and His Music. Alain Locke, Arno Press and the
    New York Times,, New York, 1969

Black Popular Music in America. Arnold Shaw, Schirmer
    Books, New York, 1986

The Face of Black Music. Valerie Wilmer and Archie Stepps,
    Da Capo Press, New York, 1976

I Remember — 80 Years of Black Entertainment, Big Bands
    and the Blues. Clyde E. B. Bernhardt, University of
    Pennsylvania Press, Philadelphia, 1986

Readings in Black American Music. Eileen Southern, ed., W.
    W. Norton & Co., Inc., 1971

Talking to Myself. Pearl Bailey, Harcourt Brace Jovanovich
    Inc., 1971

Giants of Black Music. Pauline Rivelli and Robert Levin, Da
    Capo Paperback, 1979

Bibliography

Temptations. Otis Williams, G. P. Putnam's Sons, New York, 1988

Black American Music. Hildred Roach, Crescendo Publishing Co., Boston, 1973

The Music of Black Americans. Eileen Southern, W. W. Norton & Co., Inc., New York, 1983

American Women in Jazz: 1900 to the Present. Sally Blacksin, Wideview Books, 1982

Swing Out: Great Negro Dance Bands. Gene Fernett, Pendell Publishing Co., Midland, MI, 1970

Michael Jackson, Body and Soul. Geoff Brown, Beaufort Books, New York, 1984

Greenwood Encyclopedia of Black Music: Biographical Dictionary of Afro-American and African Musicians. Eileen Southern, Greenwood Press, Westport, CT, and London, England, 1982

The Negro Almanac for 1983. John Wiley & Sons, Inc.

Dream Girl: My Life as a Supreme. Mary Wilson, St. Martin's Press, New York, 1986

Little Richard — Quasar of Rock. Charles White, Harmony Books, New York, 1984

The Illustrated Encyclopedia of Black Music. Howard A. DeWitt, Pierian Press, 1985

Ella. Sid Colin, Elm Tree Books, New York, 1987

All the Years of American Popular Music. David Eden, Prentice-Hall, Inc., 1977

Celebrating Bird: The Triumph of Charlie Parker. Gary Giddins, Beech Tree Books, New York, 1987

Jelly Roll, Jabbo and Fats. Whitney Balliett, Oxford University Press, New York, 1983

Jazz Matters — Reflections on the Music and Some of Its Makers. Doug Ramsey, University of Arkansas Press, 1989

Blacks in Classical Music. Raoul Abdul, Dodd, Mead & Co., New York, 1977

Just Mahalia, Baby. Laurraine Gorean, Word Books, Waco, TX, 1975

Count Basie. Alun Morgan, Hippocrene Books, Inc., New York, 1985

Dizzy Gillespie. Raymond Horricks, Hippocrene Books, Inc., New York, 1984

Duke Ellington. Barry Ulanov, Da Capo Books, New York, 1975

His Eye is on the Sparrow. Ethel Waters and Charles Samuels, Doubleday & Co., New York, 1951

Lena. James Hoskins, Stern and Day, 1984

Scott Joplin and the Ragtime Era. Peter Gammond, St. Martins Press, New York, 1975

The Art of Jazz — Ragtime to Be Bop. Marin Williams, ed., Da Capo Paperback, Da Capo Press, Inc., 1959

Ragtime: A Musical and Cultural History. Edward A. Berlin, University of California Press, 1980

American Musicians: 56 Portraits in Jazz. Whitney Balliet, Oxford University Press, 1986

Jazzmen. Ramsey and Smith, Harcourt Brace & Co., New York, 1939

Father of the Blues. Arna Bontemps, ed., De Capo Press, New York, 1985

Bibliography

Blues People. Le Roi Jones, Morrow Quill Paperback, New York, 1963

Echoes of Africa. Beatrice Landex, Van Rees Press, New York, 1961

Generous use was made of:

       Encyclopedia Britannica

       Encyclopedia Americana

       Academic American Encyclopedia

       Time Magazine

       Newsweek Magazine

       New York Magazine

       Washington Post

       New York Times

       People Magazine

       Parade Magazine

Index

Index

Index

Index

Index

Index

Index

Books about
African-American Achievements in History

Black Inventors of America, McKinley Burt Jr., copyright 1969,1989,
ISBN 0-89420-095-X, stock # 296959, $11.95

Black Scientists of America, Richard X. Donovan, copyright 1990,
ISBN 0-89420-265-0, stock # 297000, $10.95

Black Musicians of America, Richard X. Donovan, copyright 1991,
ISBN 0-89420-271-5, stock # 297059, $13.95

Black Americans in Defense of their Nation, Mark R. Salser, copyright 1992,
ISBN 0-89420-272-3, stock # 297130, $14.95

Black Americans in Congress, Mark R. Salser, copyright 1991,
ISBN 0-89420-273-1, stock # 297150, $14.95

Prepay by Check or Money Order:
Include $2.00 per copy for postage ($3.00 for UPS delivery, no PO Boxes)
Quantity orders – call for discounts & shipping charges

VISA, MasterCard, American Express or Discover
Call (800) 827-2499 to order

Purchase Orders:
accepted from Libraries, other Educational institutions and qualified resellers

available from:

National Book Company
PO Box 8795
Portland OR 97207-8795
(503) 228-6345